NEW DAWN A DIFFERENT SKY

NEW DAWN A DIFFERENT SKY

Navigating the Immigrant Experience

Lawrence Thompson

Published by Lawrence Thompson
First Edition: April 2025
ISBN:

DEDICATION

To the world leaders, politicians, corporations, and government parastatals: may this book serve as a reminder of the human cost of your policies and a catalyst for creating a more just and equitable world for all.

To the immigrant, the brave soul who dared to dream a different dream, may these pages offer solace, solidarity, and the strength to continue your journey.

To the one who has not immigrated, may this book foster empathy, understanding, and a recognition of the shared humanity that binds us all, regardless of borders.

In the hope that this "New Dawn" will illuminate a path towards a future where every human being can thrive, regardless of where they were born.

SEEDS IN NEW SOIL

Seeds carried on the wind's embrace,
Across the borders, time, and space.
Planted in a soil unknown,
Where roots must grow, and dreams are sown.
They weather storms, and face the cold,
Their stories whispered, to be told.
Of homelands left, and futures sought,
A new beginning dearly bought.
They blossom slowly, strong and tall,
Their vibrant colours, answering the call.
A testament to strength and will,
Their purpose to fulfil.
Though different blooms may line the way,
They share the sunshine of a brighter day.
And in their growth, a lesson lies,
Of resilience 'neath new skies.

INTRODUCTION

I remember the day I stepped off the plane, a whirlwind of emotions swirling within me. Excitement, fear, and a touch of uncertainty painted my face. The air was thick with the promise of a new life, but also the weight of the unknown. Little did I know, this was just the beginning of a journey filled with both immense challenges and unexpected joys.

What does it mean to leave behind everything you've ever known? To uproot your life, your culture, and your identity? For millions of immigrants around the world, this is not a hypothetical question, but a harsh reality. Every year, countless individuals embark on a perilous journey, leaving behind their homelands in search of a better future. They cross borders, oceans, and deserts, driven by a desire for safety, opportunity, and a chance to build a new life. Yet, this journey is fraught with challenges that can be both physical and psychological.

This book delves into the multifaceted challenges and triumphs of immigrants, shedding light on the often-overlooked struggles they encounter while adapting to a new culture and society. Through personal narratives, expert analysis, and historical context, "New Dawn, A Different Sky" aims to foster empathy, understanding, and support for immigrant communities worldwide.

To the one who hasn't immigrated

It is hard to fully grasp what it is like to leave everything we know behind, to start over in a new country where we don't speak the language or know the customs. It is a leap of faith, filled with both hope and uncertainty. Imagine having to rebuild our lives from scratch, facing language barriers, navigating unfamiliar systems, and dealing with the lingering worry of whether you will ever truly belong. It is a journey marked by resilience, strength, and a longing for connection. I hope you can take a moment to consider the challenges immigrants face and offer understanding and support. We all deserve a chance to build a better life for ourselves and our families.

To the immigrant

I know that being an immigrant can be a challenging journey, filled with both excitement and uncertainty. But please remember, you are not alone. Millions of people have walked this path before you, and many have found incredible opportunities and built fulfilling lives. Your courage and determination are inspiring. Every step you take, every obstacle you overcome, brings you closer to your dreams. Keep your head held high, and never lose sight of the reasons why you embarked on this journey. You have the power to shape your own destiny. Embrace the challenges as opportunities for growth, and celebrate your achievements, no matter how small they may seem. Know that there are people who believe in you and support you. Reach out to your community, seek help when needed, and build a network of friends and mentors. Together, we can create a world that welcomes and celebrates diversity. Your unique perspective and experiences are valuable assets to our society.

TABLE OF CONTENTS

DEDICATION iv
SEEDS IN NEW SOIL v
INTRODUCTION vi
CHAPTER ONE 1
   THE JOURNEY BEGINS 1
CHAPTER TWO 12
   THE TIGHTROPE WALK 12
CHAPTER THREE 20
   BREAKING IN 20
CHAPTER FOUR 26
   THE STRUGGLE FOR BELONGING 26
CHAPTER FIVE 30
   THE FULL PICTURE 30
CHAPTER SIX.. 35
   THE WORLD THEIR CAMPUS 35
CHAPTER SEVEN 42
   UNLOCKING POTENTIAL 42
CHAPTER EIGHT 47
   BUILDING A NEW LIFE 47
CHAPTER NINE... 58
   WEAVING NEW TIES 58
CHAPTER TEN 67
   THE STRESS OF CHANGE 67
CHAPTER ELEVEN 72
   SEEKING HELP... 72
CHAPTER TWELVE... 76

RESILIENCE AND HOPE...76
CHAPTER THIRTEEN...82
THE MANY LAYERS OF US 82
CHAPTER FOURTEEN 87
THE CONTRIBUTIONS OF IMMIGRANTS 87
CHAPTER FIFTEEN..95
VOICES THROUGH THE JOURNEY 95
CHAPTER SIXTEEN 102
POLICY RECOMMENDATIONS..............................102
CHAPTER SEVENTEEN..105
A CALL TO ACTION 105
CHAPTER EIGHTEEN...107
THE LANGUAGE OF THE HEART...........................107
CHAPTER NINETEEN...108
LETTERS TO MY FAMILY 108
CHAPTER TWENTY..113
LETTERS FROM HOME...113
CHAPTER TWENTY-ONE 116
RESOURCES AND SUPPORT 116
CONCLUSION 121
ACKNOWLEDGEMENT 124
ABOUT THE AUTHOR 125

CHAPTER ONE

THE JOURNEY BEGINS

I magine the world as a giant, breathing organism. Within it, billions of lives pulse, each a miniature story etched onto the map. Now, picture lines drawn across that map—invisible threads stretched taut between continents, countries, and even neighbouring towns. These are the pathways of migration, the routes forged by humanity's relentless movement across the globe. But what whispers drive these monumental shifts? What forces, both subtle and seismic, propel individuals and entire communities to uproot themselves and embark on journeys into the unknown? To understand migration, we must venture beyond simplistic narratives of economic gain and political flight. We must become cartographers of the heart's true drivers, tracing the intricate network of motivations that fuel this fundamental aspect of our shared history. For migration is not merely about statistics and border policies; it is about dreams and desperation, resilience and reinvention, the primal human urge to survive and, even more, to thrive.

Let's start with the bedrock motivation, the engine that has powered human movement since the dawn of time: economic necessity. It's a stark, undeniable truth that the pursuit of a better livelihood is the primary catalyst for a vast swathe of global migration. Think of the farmer whose land has become barren, unable to yield sustenance in the face of climate change or unsustainable agricultural practices. Imagine the factory worker in a declining industrial town, facing unemployment as automation and globalization reshape the economic landscape. These are not abstract figures; they are faces, stories etched with the gnawing hunger of uncertainty and the burning desire to provide for their families.

Economic migration isn't solely about escaping poverty, though that is undeniably a powerful driver. It's also about aspiration, the yearning for opportunity that whispers promises of a brighter future. Consider the skilled engineer from a developing nation, seeking to contribute their expertise in a country where innovation thrives, and their potential can be fully realised. Or the ambitious entrepreneur, chasing the dynamism of an active urban centre where capital and markets converge. These individuals are not fleeing hardship; they are actively seeking advancement, driven by a potent cocktail of ambition and the innate impulse to improve one's lot in life. The allure of economic opportunity manifests in myriad ways: the promise of higher wages to send remittances back home, the availability of jobs in sectors experiencing labour shortages, the chance to acquire skills and build a career in industries with greater growth prospects. This "pull" factor is often intertwined with "push" factors in the origin country – stagnant economies, limited social mobility, lack of investment in infrastructure and education. Migration, in this context, becomes a rational, even courageous, response to structural inequalities, a powerful act of agency in the face of widespread limitations.

However, delve deeper and we uncover motivations that are far more urgent, more primal: the desperate flight for political asylum. This is migration born not of aspiration, but of sheer, unyielding terror. Imagine the journalist silenced by a repressive regime, their voice a threat to those in power. Picture the ethnic minority facing orchestrated persecution, their very identity targeted for erasure. Envision the activist fighting for human rights, suddenly deemed an enemy of the state, their life hanging in the balance. Political asylum migration is not a choice; it is a desperate gamble for survival. It is the heart-wrenching decision to leave behind everything familiar- home, community, language, culture – in order to escape imminent danger. The motivations here are not driven by economic calculus, but by the visceral need for safety, the fundamental human right to live free from fear of violence, imprisonment, or death.

The tapestry of political asylum reveals a history of conflict, oppression, and the collapse of the rule of law. Wars and civil unrest tear societies apart, forcing populations to flee their homes in search of refuge from bombs, bullets, and brutal realities. Authoritarian regimes crush dissent, leaving no space for opposition or freedom of expression, pushing those who dare to speak out into exile. Methodical discrimination based on ethnicity, religion, sexual orientation, or political affiliation creates intolerable conditions, making migration the only viable option for those targeted. It's crucial to understand that political asylum is not simply about seeking a better life; it is about seeking life itself. Those fleeing for political reasons are often traumatized, carrying invisible wounds of violence and persecution. They are not seeking handouts; they are seeking sanctuary, a safe haven where they can rebuild their shattered lives and reclaim their dignity.

It is important to note that migration in its entirety is far richer and more sensitive than a simple dichotomy of economic necessity versus political asylum. Often, these motivations are marked together, creating complex and multi-layered journeys. Consider the case of environmental migrants, forced to abandon their homes due to climate change-induced disasters- rising sea levels, desertification, extreme weather events. While the foremost displacement might be triggered by environmental factors, their subsequent migration often becomes intertwined with economic considerations as they seek new livelihoods and integrate into new communities. Similarly, economic hardship can exacerbate political instability, creating a vicious cycle where economic migrants might also become de facto political refugees as their countries descend into conflict and chaos.

Furthermore, we cannot overlook the inmost personal and social motivations that influence migration. The desire for family reunification is a powerful force, driving individuals to cross borders to join loved ones who have already migrated. The pursuit of education, seeking access to world-class universities and diverse learning environments, propels students across continents. Even the simple innate desire for adventure, for experiencing new cultures and broadening one's horizons, plays a role in shaping migration patterns.

Exploring the motivations behind migration is not simply an academic exercise; it's an act of empathy and understanding. By recognising the factors that motivate individuals to move, we can engage with the reality and dimensions of migration in a more informed and compassionate way. It allows us to see beyond borders and statistics, and to recognise the shared humanity that binds us all. When we understand the economic anxieties that fuel the search for opportunity, the political terrors that propel the desperate flight for asylum, and the personal aspirations that shape individual journeys, we can begin to build more humane and effective responses to migration. We can craft policies that are not based on fear and exclusion, but on understanding and solidarity. We can foster societies that are welcoming and inclusive, recognising the immense potential and contributions that migrants bring.

The great human shuffle is not a problem to be solved, but a fundamental aspect of our shared story as people. By unravelling the elements of motivation, we can begin to appreciate the immense resilience, courage, and hope that fuels this continuous movement, and build a world where migration is not a forced necessity for some, but a positive and enriching experience for all. Let us not see migrants as mere numbers, but as individuals driven by dreams and fears, as reflections of our own complex and ever-evolving humanity.

Why We Leave

Imagine a life where every sunrise brings the same struggle: empty plates, a roof that leaks, and the persistent fear of what tomorrow might bring. Now imagine a whisper on the wind – a rumour of opportunity, of a place where dreams might actually blossom. This, in a nutshell, is the driving force behind many human migrations: economic necessity. We are talking about people fleeing poverty, seeking better wages, and chasing the elusive dream of a life where their children won't go hungry. They're the farmhands who leave drought-stricken fields for the promise of factory jobs, the entrepreneurs who brave uncertain waters to build businesses in new lands, and the families who risk everything to escape a debt.

But economic hardship is just one piece of the puzzle. Sometimes, the reason for leaving is not about what you lack, but about what you fear. This is where political asylum comes in. In this reality, your voice is not your own, your beliefs are punishable offences, and your very existence hangs in the balance. The government you once trusted has become your enemy, and your only hope lies in escaping the suffocating grip of oppression. These are the refugees- the dissidents, the minorities, the victims of war and persecution. They flee not for fortune, but for survival. They seek sanctuary, a place where they can breathe freely, think freely, and live without the spectre of fear.

Of course, the reality of migration is rarely this simple. Often, economic desperation, political fear, and the enduring universal desire for a better life create an intense situation. Some may leave for economic reasons, only to find themselves caught in the crossfire of a political conflict. Others may flee persecution but find themselves struggling to survive in a foreign land, grappling with language barriers and cultural differences. But despite the challenges, the enduring spirit prevails. Migrants, whether driven by economic need or political fear, are ultimately seeking the same thing: a chance to build a future, to play a role in society, and to live a life filled with dignity and hope. So next time you see someone from a different background, remember the story they might carry, the journey that led them to your corner of the world.

Let's delve into the lives of a few individuals whose stories illustrate the intricacies, challenges, and triumphs of this global phenomenon.

Amina's Odyssey

Her heart pounded like a drumbeat in her chest. The worn leather of her backpack felt like Armour against the world. Amina was not just leaving her village in Syria; she was leaving everything she knew. War had painted her home in shades of fear and uncertainty, and the whispers of a better life across the Mediterranean Sea were too loud to ignore. The experience of the journey consisted of the fluctuation between hope and despair. She joined a caravan of strangers, their faces etched with the same determination. Days turned into nights as they trekked through barren landscapes, the sun beating down on their weary bodies. Hunger gnawed at their bellies, and thirst parched their throats. Yet, they pressed on, fuelled by the dream of a future beyond the horizon.

The sea, once a distant glimmer, loomed large before them. A rickety boat, barely afloat, was their vessel of hope. Amina's breath hitched as she boarded, the weight of her dreams and fears heavy upon her shoulders. The engine roared to life, and they were swallowed by the vast expanse of blue. The Mediterranean was a tempestuous mistress. Waves crashed against the boat, threatening to capsize it. Amina's stomach churned, but her grip on the side of the boat tightened. The screams of others mingled with the roar of the engine, a symphony of terror and desperation. Days turned into nights, and nights into days. The horizon was an unyielding companion, promising a land of safety and opportunity.

Finally, a distant light appeared, a symbol of hope in the darkness. As they neared the shore, the cheers of welcome washed over them, a much-needed reprieve from the horrors they had endured. Amina stepped onto European soil, her feet sinking into the cool earth. The taste of freedom was bittersweet, a victory hard-won. She had left behind a life shattered by war, carrying with her the scars of a journey that had tested her spirit to its limits. Yet, in her eyes, a flicker of hope remained, a testament to the indomitable human spirit that can endure even the harshest of trials. Now, in a new country, she's rebuilding her life, pursuing education, and dreaming of a future filled with hope.

Carlos's American Dream

Dreams weren't in Carlos's blood; the soil was. He was born to be a farmer, like his father and his father before him. But the fields of his small village in Mexico offered little more than backbreaking work and meagre pay. The whispers of a land of opportunity, a place called America, filled his ears. It was a gamble, a leap into the unknown, but the promise of a better life was too enticing to ignore. With an inner turmoil of hope and pockets full of desperation, Carlos boarded a rickety bus bound for the border. The journey was a blur of dusty roads and anxious faces. Days turned into nights, and nights into days, as the bus wound its way through the unforgiving desert. Finally, they reached the wall, a towering monolith that separated hope from despair. With the help of a coyote, a shadowy figure who guided migrants across the border, Carlos slipped through the gaps in the wall. He emerged into a world bathed in the harsh light of the American sun. It was a world of endless possibilities, but also of immense quagmires.

Carlos found work in a tomato field, stooping under the scorching sun, his back aching, his hands blistered. The pay was barely enough to survive, but it was a start. He saved every penny, dreaming of a day when he could afford to rent a room, a place to call his own. The relentless march of time saw Carlos bounce from one unpromising field to the next, each job a fleeting, unfulfilling experience. He learned English, a language that opened doors, but also closed them. He faced discrimination, prejudice, and the unremitting threat of deportation. Yet, he persevered, spurred by an unwavering belief in the American Dream.

Then, an opportunity arose. A small business, a taco stand, was up for sale. It was a chance to be his own boss, to build something of his own. With borrowed money and a lot of hard work, Carlos bought the stand. He devoted himself entirely to it, creating a taste of Mexico in the heart of America. The taco stand became a success. People lined up for blocks, drawn by the authentic flavours and Carlos's warm smile. He hired workers, expanded his business, and finally, he was able to buy a house, a symbol of his hard-earned American Dream.

Carlos's path was not easy. It was filled with hardship, sacrifice, and uncertainty. But it was also a journey of unshakeable faith in a better future. His story is proof of the power of the human spirit, and serves as a noteworthy message that the American

Dream, though elusive, is still within reach for those who dare to chase it.

Sun-Hee's Silent Struggle

Brimming with dreams, Sun-Hee, a young woman, bid farewell to her beloved Korea in the early 1970s. The promise of a better life in the United States had lured her across the vast Pacific Ocean. Yet, as she stepped onto American soil, she soon realised that the reality was far from the idyllic picture she had painted in her mind. Early on, culture shock was intense. The linguistic divide, the unfamiliar customs, and the relentless pace of American life were all foreign and intimidating. Sun-Hee found herself isolated, a silent observer in a world that seemed to move at a dizzying speed. Even with everything stacked against her, she was determined to make a life for herself in this new land. She enrolled in language classes, tirelessly practicing her English pronunciation. The lessons were tough, but she persevered, fuelled by the hope of a brighter future. As she gradually mastered the language, Sun-Hee began to venture out of her comfort zone. She took part-time jobs, working long hours in factories and restaurants. The physical labour was exhausting, but it imbued her with a sense of purpose and financial independence. Yet, even as she made progress, loneliness gnawed at her. She missed her family, her friends, and the familiar sights and sounds of Korea. Homesickness often crept in, a heavy cloud over her.

One day, while browsing through a local bookstore, the woman stumbled upon a book about Korean immigrants in America. The stories resonated with her intimately, making her feel less alone in her struggles. Inspired by these stories, she decided to join a Korean community centre. At the centre, Sun-Hee found a haven. She met other Korean immigrants who shared her experiences and aspirations. They formed a tight-knit group, supporting each other through thick and thin. Together, they celebrated Korean holidays, cooked traditional Korean dishes, and shared stories of their homeland. Through her involvement with the community centre, Sun-Hee's confidence grew. She started volunteering, helping newcomers navigate the variations of American life. She also joined a Korean dance group, finding joy and expression in the rhythmic movements.

Years later, Sun-Hee's life in America took shape. She had a stable job, a loving family, and a strong network of friends. The challenges she had faced had shaped her into a tenacious and compassionate woman.

Leaving Home- My Escape from Stagnation

The air in Lagos hung heavy, thick with the scent of exhaust fumes and the looming shadow of what could have been. I, like so many others, yearned for something more – a chance to escape the suffocating grip of poverty and the continuous stifling administrations that choked progress. Nigeria, my vibrant, chaotic, beloved Nigeria, faded into a patchwork of memories below.

Lagos, with its relentless energy, was where my story began. I loved the busy markets, the sound of hawkers calling out their wares, the smoky aroma of suya sizzling on roadside grills. But even amidst the beauty, a gnawing unease settled in my soul. The erratic power supply, a metaphor for the instability that plagued our lives, was an incessant source of frustration. Businesses struggled, dreams were stifled, and the hum of generators became the soundtrack of our lives. Then there was the insecurity. News of kidnappings and robberies was a daily occurrence. Fear became a shadow that lurked in every corner, stealing our joy and our sense of safety. Even my own family was not spared; we lost a cousin to an unprovoked act of violence, a wound that never fully healed. Education, the supposed ladder to a better future, was a broken promise. Overcrowded classrooms, underpaid teachers, and a crumbling infrastructure left many, including myself, with a subpar education. The allure of foreign universities, with their promise of quality education and a brighter future, became an irresistible siren song. But perhaps the most insidious of all was the lack of opportunity. I had a good degree, but jobs were scarce, and those that existed often demanded bribes or connections I simply did not have. I watched my friends, bright and ambitious, wither away, their potential crushed by a system that seemed designed to hold them back.

The United Kingdom, with its promise of stability, security, and opportunity, became a magnet of hope. It was not an easy decision. Leaving my family, my friends, the familiar cadence of my life, felt like tearing a piece of myself away. But the promise of a better life, a life where my talents could flourish, where my dreams would not be crushed by ingrained failures, was a force too powerful to resist. I knew I had to try. I had to see if I could build a better future, not just for myself, but someday, perhaps, for those I left behind.

This is not just my story, but the story of millions of Nigerians who have made the difficult decision to leave their homeland in search of a better life, each with their own story of struggle and hope. We were all chasing a dream, a dream of a life where hard work was rewarded, where safety wasn't a luxury, and where our potential could finally take flight.

Understanding the "Why"

Understanding the motivations behind migration is crucial. It helps us move past the easy division of "us" versus "them" and fosters empathy for the human experience. It allows us to see the world through the eyes of those who have been forced to leave everything they know behind, to embark on a perilous journey in search of a better tomorrow.

CHAPTER TWO

THE TIGHTROPE WALK

T he day I left, Harmattan haze clung to Lagos like a second skin. It was a fitting farewell, an emblem of the familiar I was leaving behind for the unknown. My dream, like that of many Nigerians, was London, a land of opportunities, or so I had been told. My carefully packed suitcase held not just clothes and cherished photos, but also the gravity of expectations- mine, my family's, my community's.

The first hurdle was the visa application. A mountain of paperwork, each document evidence of the intricate web of United Kingdom immigration law. Bank statements, proof of accommodation, letters of sponsorship- each scrutinised, each a potential landmine. The anxiety was an unrelenting hum beneath my skin. What if they did not believe I would return? What if a single missing document shattered my dreams? Then came the interview at the embassy. Every question felt like a test, my answers weighed and measured. The interviewer's gaze was impassive, revealing nothing. It was a performance, and my future hung in the balance. When the visa was finally granted, it felt like winning a lottery, a golden ticket to a new life.

Touching down at Heathrow, I felt the crisp and cold air - a dramatic difference to the Lagos heat. But the physical chill was nothing compared to the emotional one that soon settled in. London was tremendous, indifferent. The Underground map was a multicoloured spiderweb, the accents a confusing jumble. I was adrift in a sea of faces, each hurrying past, oblivious to my existence. Finding a place to live was a nightmare. Landlords were hesitant to rent to a newcomer with no credit history, no local references. Every rejection was a blow, chipping away at my resolve. I bounced between temporary accommodations, each a fresh indicator of my precarious situation. The search for a job was equally demoralising. My Nigerian qualifications were met with polite indifference. "You have no UK experience," was the repeated phrase. I took any job I could find -cleaning, delivery, anything to make ends meet. Each menial task felt like a betrayal of the hopes I had carried with me. The process seemed never-ending. National Insurance number, bank account, registration with the local council – each step was a battle against red tape, endless forms, and long queues. I felt like a ghost, invisible yet perpetually under scrutiny.

Loneliness became my unwelcome companion. I missed the vibrant chaos of Lagos, the easy camaraderie of my friends, the warmth of my family. The calls home became my lifeline, but they also brought a pang of guilt. Had I made a mistake? Was this lonely struggle worth it? Yet, amidst the hardship, there were moments of grace. A kind word from a stranger, a shared laugh with a colleague, the discovery of a small Nigerian shop tucked away in a corner of the city. These small moments of connection were like sparks in the darkness, reminding me that I was not alone.

My journey to the United Kingdom has been a trial by fire. It has tested my mettle, my patience, the very foundations of who I thought I was. But it has also shown me the strength I never knew I had. I am still navigating the complexity of this new life, still finding my place in this city. But I am here. I have survived. And that, in itself, is a victory. Immigration is not just about paperwork and visas. It is about navigating a new culture, grappling with identity, and balancing both loss and hope. It is a journey that transforms, scars, and ultimately, defines.

This is just one perspective, and the immigrant experience is incredibly diverse. Each individual's journey is unique, shaped by their background, circumstances, and personal fortitude.

Navigating the Legal Complex

The first, and arguably most formidable, impediment in the immigration process is the legal systems erected by nation-states. Immigration law, often a dense and ever-evolving body of legislation, presents a grave challenge even for seasoned legal professionals, let alone individuals often unfamiliar with the host country's language and legal apparatus. This legal landscape begins with the extensive variety of visa categories; immigration is seldom a single pathway, but rather segmented into a bewildering array of categories, each with meticulously defined eligibility criteria. From skilled worker visas to family reunification permits, student visas to asylum claims, each demands specific qualifications, documentation, and adherence to often opaque procedures. Understanding which category, if any, aligns with an individual's unique circumstances becomes a daunting task. For instance, skilled worker visas frequently prioritise specific professions and educational backgrounds, overlooking those with valuable skills acquired through non-traditional avenues. Even family reunification, while seemingly straightforward, can be hindered by stringent definitions of "family" and intricate evidentiary requirements.

Adding to this are the onerous and ever-shifting eligibility criteria. Even within a specific visa category, the requirements are rarely static. Governments frequently adjust these criteria based on perceived economic needs, security concerns, and shifting political considerations. This continual flux cultivates a climate of uncertainty, potentially rendering meticulously prepared applications suddenly obsolete. Factors such as age, health, monetary assets, criminal history, even minor past infractions, and perceived "likelihood of integration" are often scrutinised subjectively, leaving applicants feeling judged against an arbitrary and unattainable ideal.

Compounding this further is the application gauntlet itself, designed as a rigorous test of perseverance. Applicants are required to amass enormous quantities of documentation, often stretching back years, proving identity, qualifications, relationships, and intentions. This can involve retrieving birth certificates from remote villages, translating documents into multiple languages, obtaining police clearances from various jurisdictions, and the dilemmas of engaging with the distinct governmental mechanisms of numerous countries all at once. Seemingly simple documents can become insurmountable obstacles when operational inefficiencies, lack of access to archives, or political instability in the applicant's country of origin are considered. Moreover, the demand for meticulous disclosure can feel particularly intrusive, requiring revelation of highly private information, medical histories, and financial details, often without clear understanding of data usage and protection.

Effectively conducting legal proceedings within this intricate system often necessitates legal representation. Immigration lawyers possess specialised knowledge and provide invaluable guidance in application preparation, document gathering, and appeals representation. However, legal representation is often prohibitive for individuals already facing financial precarity when considering immigration. This creates a system where access to legal expertise become another constraint, disproportionately affecting vulnerable populations.

Even with meticulous preparation, visa applications can face rejection, casting a shadow of uncertainty and appeal. Reasons for rejection are frequently vague, lacking specifics or clear redress pathways. While appeal processes exist, they are often lengthy, costly, and without guaranteed success. The ever-present threat of rejection, and the uncertainty surrounding appeals, can trap applicants in a prolonged state of limbo, delaying life plans, disrupting current lives, and fuelling severe anxieties about the future.

A System of Delays, Red Tape, and Impersonality

Beyond the initial legal hurdles, the immigration process is further toughened by the official channels responsible for its administration. These systems, often insufficiently funded, swamped by volume, and characterised by opaque procedures, are a major cause of the frustrations and anxieties experienced by immigrants.

One of the most universally cited issues is protracted processing times. Applications can languish for months, even years, with minimal or no communication regarding their status, effectively placing life on hold. This prolonged uncertainty casts a long shadow, compelling applicants to defer major life decisions, from employment and education to family planning and housing. The excessive length of this process, combined with a lack of transparency, can breed despair and a perception of powerlessness when faced with an impersonal and unresponsive system.

Adding to this, applicants are required to deal with a confusing multi-agency process. Immigration processes frequently involve dealings with multiple government agencies, each possessing its own distinct procedures, timelines, and communication channels. Applicants may need to engage with immigration departments, embassies or consulates, labour ministries, healthcare providers, and security agencies, often with limited coordination between them. This fragmented framework places the burden squarely on the applicant to navigate these disconnected entities, track progress across different agencies, and ensure all necessary information reaches each, often without clear guidance or a central point of contact.

The tyranny of documentation and verification further complicates matters, as application procedures often rely heavily on excessive documentation and redundant verification layers. Applicants may be asked to repeatedly submit identical documents, respond to repetitive information requests, and navigate cumbersome online portals or paper-based methods. The focus on minute details, coupled with rigid procedural adherence, can feel arbitrary and dehumanising, particularly when combined with language barriers or limited access to technology. The sheer volume of paperwork and the seemingly endless requests for verification result in a feeling of being lost and individual needs are overshadowed by procedural compliance.

Communication breakdowns and a lack of transparency further exacerbate the situation, as that from immigration authorities is often vague, infrequent, and furnishes limited opportunities for clarification or personal engagement. Applicants frequently grapple with understanding their application status, the reasons for delays, or the specific steps needed to move forward. Decisions often appear to be made within a "black box," lacking transparency regarding the criteria used or the decision-making process itself. This lack of clear communication and transparency fosters mistrust and reinforces feelings of powerlessness and alienation within the regulatory system.

Despite the emphasis on standardised procedures, inconsistent application of rules and procedures can create arbitrariness and disparity. Different caseworkers may interpret regulations in varying ways, leading to disparate outcomes for applicants in similar situations. This lack of consistency and predictability undermines trust in the system and amplifies anxieties about unfair treatment. Geographic variations in processing times and outcomes, often reflecting regional resource allocation and political priorities, further highlight the inherent arbitrariness and disparity within many immigration systems.

The immigration process is not merely a legal or bureaucratic matter; it is an emotive experience that touches upon the lives of millions of people around the world. It is a journey that demands not only legal expertise and bureaucratic proficiency but also empathy, understanding, and a recognition of the emotional toll that the process can take.

The Invisible Backpack

We, immigrants, carry an invisible backpack. It's not a physical thing, easily seen or understood, but it's there, strapped to our shoulders every single day. And it is heavy, unbelievably heavy. Inside, it is packed tight with anxieties, uncertainties, and the unspoken burden of a thousand expectations – the things we carry that no one else can see, but that define so much of our journey. Leaving behind everything familiar – our familiar – is the first thing we pack into that unseen burden. The scent of grandmother's cooking fades from memory, the echoes of childhood friends' laughter grow faint, the comforting rhythms of our native tongue become a distant song. It's a shattering loss, a severing, like leaving behind a part of ourselves, leaving a raw, aching void where belonging once resided.

Stepping into a new land, even one brimming with promise, often means entering a space that feels viscerally alien, intensely isolating. The impassable language rises before us like an insurmountable wall, leaving us unheard, misunderstood, adrift in a sea of unfamiliar sounds. Cultural differences, sometimes subtle, often jarring, weave their way into every exchange, leading to awkward silences, unintentional micro-aggressions, and an exhausting awareness that we are walking on eggshells, never quite sure of our footing. Fear becomes an unwelcome companion in our invisible backpack. Fear of failure – will we make it here? Fear of deportation – will we be allowed to stay? Fear of not being able to provide, to protect the families we have brought with us, or the ones we hope to build. The pressure to succeed, to assimilate, to prove our worthiness of this new place, this new chance – it's immense, a crushing load that presses down on us constantly. This relentless pressure doesn't just stay in our minds; it manifests in our bodies, surfacing as anxiety that gnaws at our insides, depression that darkens our days, even physical ailments that betray the strain we are under.

But within this heavy backpack, nestled amongst the hardships, are also the unexpected treasures of buoyancy, the streaks of unforeseen joy. The kindness of strangers, a helping hand offered when we least anticipate it, the unexpected support of a newfound community built from shared experiences – these moments are like rays of sunshine breaking through the clouds. They offer glimmers of hope, affirm our own inner strength, and reveal the enduring power of the human spirit that resides within each of us. The quiet pride of overcoming seemingly impossible obstacles, and the small victories that accumulate, form a feeling of achievement. These are the unexpected rewards that lighten the load, if only for a moment. The immigrant journey is defined by both immense challenges and unexpected, profound rewards.

Understanding this invisible backpack, recognising the unseen weight we carry, is essential. It allows you to truly see us, to empathise with our struggles, to appreciate our stamina, and to celebrate not just our triumphs, but our very presence, our enduring contribution to the world. It's a story not just of hardship, but of courage, of hope, and of our unbreakable will to come into our own, to build a better future, for ourselves and for generations to come.

CHAPTER THREE

BREAKING IN

K abita's knuckles were white as she clutched her shopping list, her only guide in the overwhelming chaos of the American supermarket. Her first week in Chicago had been a whirlwind of confusing street signs and baffling food labels. Today's mission: acquire "a dozen eggs." Easy, right? Kabita, used to buying eggs loose from a local farmer back home, stared in bewilderment at the overwhelming wall of cartons. "Extra-large," "jumbo," "cage-free," "organic"... were these different species of eggs? She finally grabbed a carton at random, hoping for the best. Later, attempting to bake a cake, she discovered her "dozen" contained eighteen eggs. Clearly, "dozen" had a different meaning here.

Elsewhere in the city, Javier was having his own adventure. He'd landed a job as a delivery driver, but his English was still a work in progress. His GPS, bless its robotic brain, directed him to "18th Street." Javier, diligently following its instructions, drove up and down 18th Street for an hour, unable to find the designated address. Finally, in exasperation, he called his boss.
"I cannot find the building!" he exclaimed. "It is on Eighteenth Street, but I have been on it many times!"

His boss, after a moment of confused silence, realised the problem.
"Javier," he chuckled, "it's '18th,' not 'Eighteenth.' It's a number, not the whole word!"

Anika clutched her umbrella, a flimsy shield against the relentless drizzle. Her first week in London had been a masterclass in deciphering cryptic phrases like "bits and bobs" and "cheeky Nando's." Today's mission: navigating the Tube. Anika, used to her city's orderly metro layout, stared in bewilderment at the map, a chaotic dance of coloured lines.
"Mind the gap," a disembodied voice boomed, just as she tripped, narrowly avoiding a face-plant onto a gaggle of commuters.
She finally found her platform, only to discover the train was "delayed due to leaves on the line.
" Leaves? On a train line?
Back home, leaves were a pleasant autumnal sight, not a public transportation crisis.

In South London, Rajesh was attempting to order a "cuppa" at a traditional pub. He'd diligently practiced the phrase, but the rapid-fire Cockney accent of the bartender threw him for a loop.
"Oi, guv'nor, what'll it be?" the bartender chirped.
Rajesh, panicking, blurted out the only British-sounding word he could think of.
"Sherlock Holmes!" he declared.
The bartender paused, a confused frown creasing his brow.
"Sherlock…Holmes? You want a pint of Sherlock Holmes?"
Rajesh, mortified, could only nod weakly. He ended up with a pint of bitter, which he drank with a forced smile, trying to blend in with the locals discussing the "footie."

Then there was Fatima, determined to embrace British cuisine. She'd heard tales of the legendary "full English breakfast" and decided to give it a try. The plate that arrived was a monument to fried food: sausages, bacon, eggs, tomatoes, mushrooms, toast, and... black pudding. Fatima eyed the black pudding with suspicion.

"Is... is this some kind of dessert?" she asked the waitress.

The waitress chuckled. "Nah, love. It's blood sausage."

Fatima's eyes widened. Blood sausage? She bravely took a bite. It wasn't quite what she expected, but she finished the whole plate, determined to conquer this culinary Everest.

Chika's most embarrassing moment involved public transportation. She was trying to take the Tube to a friend's house in Brixton. She studied the map, carefully planned her route, and confidently boarded the train. Several stops later, she realised something was wrong. The scenery was...not Brixton. She asked a fellow passenger for directions.

"Excuse me," she said, "is this train going to Brixton?"

The passenger looked at her, confused.

"Brixton? Love, you're on the Northern Line. Brixton's on the Victoria Line."

Chika felt her face flush. She'd gotten on the wrong train! Completely and utterly lost. She mumbled her thanks and got off at the next stop, feeling like the biggest "JJC" (Johnny Just Come) in London.

We are all just trying to figure things out, one awkward encounter at a time. And sometimes, the best way to deal with it is to laugh at ourselves. Because at the end of the day, we are all just trying to find our place in the world, one hilarious mistake at a time.

Embracing the Unknown

A new culture is like a puzzle to be solved. The language is a cryptic code, the customs are hidden clues, and the people are the enigmatic puzzle masters. You're a curious explorer, slowly piecing together the intricate patterns of this unfamiliar world.

This is the exhilarating adventure of cultural adaptation. Communication in a new land is like walking into a room where everyone is sharing a secret language. You see the smiles, hear the laughter, but the meaning remains hidden. This is what silently isolates many immigrants daily, an erosion of their sense of self as they contend with being understood, to participate, and to truly find their place. Language is not just about words; it is the vessel for our thoughts, feelings, and dreams. It is how we build relationships, negotiate, and navigate the world. When that vessel is cracked, communication becomes a minefield. Simple requests turn into frustrating charades, jokes fall flat, and the simple aspects of social interaction are lost in translation.

The impact goes beyond the practical. Misunderstandings can lead to isolation, discrimination, and even danger. A simple trip to the doctor can become a terrifying ordeal if you cannot explain your symptoms. Job interviews can be derailed by misinterpretations, and navigating bureaucracy can feel like an impossible obstacle course. But the conundrums of language barriers are not insurmountable. Learning a new language is an act of courage, a bridge built between cultures. It demonstrates the human's incredible capacity for adaptation. And while the journey may be fraught with frustration, it also offers unexpected rewards. The process of learning a new language opens doors to new perspectives, new ways of thinking, and a more enlightened understanding of life and existence. It fosters empathy and appreciation for the diverse array of languages that makes our world so rich and vibrant.

A World of Differences

Entering a world that feels both familiar and utterly foreign, an immigrant embarks on a journey of cultural adjustment. It's like being dropped into a movie halfway through, where you don't know the characters, the plot, or even the language. The simplest things become a minefield of confusion. Greetings that were once warm and familiar now feel awkward and insincere. Handshakes too firm or too limp, hugs too long or too short – every social interaction is a delicate dance where the steps are unknown. Even the most mundane tasks, like ordering food or asking for directions, become a test of courage and linguistic skill. Then there's the unspoken rules, the cultural ways that only locals seem to grasp. Is it okay to be late? How close do you stand when talking to someone? When is it appropriate to joke, and when to be serious? These invisible boundaries can lead to misunderstandings and awkward silences, leaving the immigrant feeling like an outsider, no matter how hard they try to fit in.

And let's not forget the food. The flavours, the textures, the sheer variety can be overwhelming. What was once comfort food now seems strange and unfamiliar. The immigrant may find themselves longing for the simple tastes of home, while simultaneously being expected to embrace the culinary adventures of their new country. It's a delicate balancing act, this journey of cultural adjustment. The immigrant must navigate between holding onto their heritage and embracing their new reality. It's a challenge, yes, but also an opportunity for growth and understanding.

Exiting the aircraft, I was greeted by a different kind of air. Not just the climate, but the pulse of life. It wasn't the language curb that tripped me up first, but the unspoken rules – the way people queued, the appropriate distance in a conversation, the unwritten codes of politeness. Every interaction was a minefield. Was a raised eyebrow a sign of disapproval or just a quirk of their facial expressions? Did a longer silence mean the conversation was over, or were they simply lost in thought? Small gestures, big misunderstandings. Then there were the social gatherings. The food was unfamiliar, the music foreign. Laughter echoed around me, but I couldn't quite join in. The jokes fell flat, the references were lost on me. I felt like an outsider looking in, a silent observer in a vibrant tableau. It wasn't just about fitting in, it was about finding my place. Where were the lines drawn between respecting their customs and holding onto my own? How could I bridge the gap between my past and this new reality? The journey wasn't easy, but with time, patience, and a willingness to learn, the fog began to lift. I found allies, discovered shared interests, and slowly, I started to belong. The initial challenges were steep, but they were the first steps on a path towards a new, rich, and unexpected life.

Adjusting to a new language, customs, and social norms is not easy. It takes time, patience, and a willingness to embrace the unknown. But the rewards are well worth the effort. You will gain a heightened understanding of yourself and the world around you. You will learn to appreciate the diversity of how people live and see the world. And you will emerge from this journey a more adaptable, flexible, and culturally aware individual.

CHAPTER FOUR

THE STRUGGLE FOR BELONGING

T he human experience includes a fundamental desire: the need to belong. From our earliest moments, we yearn for connection, acceptance, and our place within the world. This quest for belonging is a powerful motivator, shaping our choices, influencing our behaviours, and ultimately moulding our self-concept. Yet, for many, the path to belonging is fraught with predicaments, marked by feelings of isolation, exclusion, and the persistent struggle to find where they truly fit in.

The struggle for belonging can manifest in numerous ways. It may arise from feeling different, whether due to race, ethnicity, religion, gender identity, sexual orientation, or any other aspect of our identity that sets us apart from the perceived norm. It can stem from social anxieties, leaving us feeling awkward or inadequate in social settings. It can be triggered by life transitions, such as moving to a new city, changing schools, or experiencing a major loss. Or, it can be a consequence of institutional inequalities, where societal frameworks and biases create roadblocks to inclusion and perpetuate feelings of marginalisation.

Amira's Quest for Identity

Amira stepped off the plane, a wave of trepidation washing over her. She clutched her suitcase, a symbol of the dreams and aspirations she brought with her from Somalia. The chilly London air hit her like a slap in the face, an abrupt marker of the unfamiliar world she now stood in. As she made her way through customs, Amira's mind wandered to the life she left behind: vibrant markets, spicy aromas and warm smiles. She had traded it all for a chance at safety and success. Daily struggles in English class, rejections from part-time jobs and lonely nights in a small flat tested her resolve. Amira felt like a ghost, invisible and insignificant. Was this new life worth leaving behind the only home she knew?

On a sun-drenched afternoon, while exploring the vibrant city centre, Amira stumbled upon a small Somali café. The familiar scent of cardamom and myrrh enveloped her like a warm hug. She pushed open the door, revealing a cozy space filled with the comforting sounds of her native language. Amira felt a lump form in her throat as she ordered a cup of spiced tea. The owner, an elderly Somali woman named Khadija, struck up a conversation. Amira opened up about her struggles, her fears and her dreams. Khadija listened attentively, nodding along.
"You are not alone, child," she said.
"We have all been where you are. Our journey is not just about geography; it's about finding pieces of ourselves."
The woman's words struck a chord. Amira realised she wasn't alone. There were others like her whose collective story flowed into the river that defined this cosmopolitan city.

She started attending community events, language exchange programs and cultural festivals. With each connection, Amira's conviction of belonging grew. At an art exhibition, she met Jamal, a Somali-British artist. His vibrant paintings depicted the immigrant experience – the struggles, the triumphs, and the resilience. Amira felt seen. They exchanged numbers, and Jamal introduced her to his circle of fellow artists and activists. Inspired, Amira enrolled in art classes. As she painted, she began to heal. Colours danced on her canvas, blending memories of Mogadishu with the gritty beauty of London. Her art became her voice, expressing the many forms of her identity. Amira's artwork quickly gained recognition. Local galleries showcased her pieces, and she was invited to speak at community events. With each platform, she shared her story, incorporating elements of her Somali heritage and her experience in British culture.

On a particular day, as she showcased her artwork, Amira met a young girl, no more than ten years old. The girl's curious gaze reminded Amira of herself when she first arrived.
"Where are you from?" the girl asked.
Amira smiled, her response no longer fraught with uncertainty.
"I am from Somalia and the UK. I am a fusion of cultures, traditions and dreams."
The girl's eyes widened.
"That's cool!" she exclaimed.
Amira chuckled, knowing she had found her place. Her identity was no longer a struggle, but a celebration – an interlacement of stories from Somalia, London and her unyielding spirit.

The Invisible Thread

An invisible thread connects us to our homeland, a lifeline of comfort and identity. But in a new land, that thread strains, threatening to snap. This is the immigrant experience: a continual tug-of-war between the familiar and the foreign, a lifelong search for belonging. It starts with the simple things: the accents that draw curious stares, the unfamiliar foods that leave us longing for the flavours of home. The holidays feel hollow without the rituals and traditions we grew up with. Loneliness creeps in, a companion in the echoing silence of our new apartment. Then there's the struggle to be seen, to be heard. Our ideas, our viewpoints, our very existence often feels invisible. We navigate a minefield of cultural practices, constantly second-guessing ourselves, wondering if we're being too loud, too quiet, too different. But amidst the quandaries, there are glimmers of hope. Acts of kindness from strangers, unexpected friendships forged across cultural divides, the thrill of discovering a hidden gem in our new city that reminds us of home. Slowly, tentatively, we begin to integrate new experiences into the evolving story of our lives. We learn the local lingo, the unspoken rules of social interaction. We discover new passions, new communities that embrace us for who we are. We start to belong, not just to the place we live, but to the person we're becoming.

The journey is not linear, not easy. There are setbacks, moments of doubt, and the occasional pang of homesickness. But with an open attitude and a willingness to embrace the unknown, we find a place where we truly belong.

CHAPTER FIVE

THE FULL PICTURE

The aroma of cumin and coriander hung heavy in the air of Mrs. Rodriguez's tiny apartment. It was the smell of home, of her childhood in Mexico, a comforting counterpoint to the gnawing anxiety that settled in her stomach each morning. Her son, Jaime, was starting kindergarten. He bounced on the balls of his feet, his backpack overflowing with crayons and a lunchbox shaped like a fire-truck. Mrs. Rodriguez smiled, trying to push aside the worry.

"Be good for your teacher, mi amor," she whispered, tucking a stray strand of hair behind his ear. "Make new friends."

Jaime, oblivious to his mother's apprehension, skipped out the door, his laughter echoing down the hallway.

The first few weeks were a blur. Jaime came home with drawings of smiling suns and stick figures. He'd chatter excitedly about his new friends, their names tripping off his tongue – Emily, Ben, Sarah. Then, things began to shift. Jaime started coming home with his head down, his lunchbox untouched.

He'd mumble about "stupid games" and "not wanting to play."

One day, he blurted out,

"They say I smell weird, Mommy. Like tacos."

Mrs. Rodriguez felt a cold dread grip her core. This was the subtle, insidious kind of discrimination – the whispered comments, the averted gazes, the exclusion from the lunch table. Overt discrimination followed soon after. A note came home from school, a polite request for a meeting. The teacher, a woman with a tight smile and a stiff posture, explained that Jaime was "disruptive" and "distracting" other students. Mrs. Rodriguez tried to defend her son, to explain that he was shy, that he was still learning English. But the teacher remained unmoved. Jaime's grades plummeted. He stopped talking at the dinner table, his eyes mirroring the sadness in his mother's.

One afternoon, while cleaning under Jaime's bed, Mrs. Rodriguez found a crumpled piece of paper. It was a drawing – a stick figure with a dark skin tone, a noose drawn around its neck. Below it, scrawled in childish handwriting, were the words:
"Go back to your country."
The world tilted on its axis. This was not a whisper, not an averted gaze. This was hate, raw and ugly, aimed at her innocent child. Mrs. Rodriguez felt a surge of anger, then a wave of despair. How could she protect her son from this invisible, insidious poison that seeped into every corner of their lives? She knew she couldn't fight this alone. She reached out to other immigrant families in the neighbourhood, families who understood the sting of discrimination, the unending battle to feel like they belonged. Together, they organised. They spoke at school board meetings, demanding changes in curriculum, demanding sensitivity training for teachers. They volunteered at the school, bridging the gap between their culture and the mainstream. The fight was long and arduous.

There were setbacks, moments of discouragement, and times when it all felt unbearable. But slowly, things began to change. Jaime started making new friends, friends who saw him for who he was – a kind, intelligent boy with a love for soccer and a passion for drawing. The school implemented a diversity program, celebrating different cultures and traditions. The air of apprehension that had hung over Mrs. Rodriguez's home began to lift. The scars remained, a lasting memento of the prejudice they had faced. But they had found their voice, their strength in unity. They had shown their son that even in the face of adversity, hope could prevail.

Even though this is just a fictional story and does not necessarily reflect the experiences of all immigrants, it illustrates how discrimination can manifest in both overt and subtle ways, impacting the lives of immigrants and their families. It highlights the importance of community, resilience, and the fight for a more inclusive and equitable society.

A Tale of Two Evils

Discrimination and prejudice are insidious forces that plague societies worldwide. They are rooted in ignorance, fear, and a fundamental failure to recognise the inherent worth and dignity of every earthborn. While often used interchangeably, they represent distinct but interconnected concepts.

Prejudice is a preconceived judgment or opinion, often negative, about an individual or group based on limited or biased information. It's an attitude, a feeling, often formed without sufficient reason or experience. Prejudice can be based on a multitude of factors, including race, ethnicity, religion, gender, sexual orientation, socioeconomic status, age, disability, and more. It exists in the realm of thought and feeling, shaping our perceptions and biases.

Discrimination, on the other hand, is the action that stems from prejudice. It involves treating individuals or groups unfairly based on their membership in a particular category. Discrimination can manifest in various forms, from subtle micro-aggressions and everyday slights to overt acts of violence and rampant oppression. It can occur in employment, housing, education, healthcare, the justice system, and virtually every facet of life.

The Impact: Skin Deep

The shared experience of discrimination is a perpetual ache, deep in the bones of every immigrant I know. We come here, to this new land, with dreams as bright as any star. We carry them like precious cargo, tucked into our hearts alongside photos of family we left behind and the recipes for dishes that taste like home. We work hard, harder than many can imagine, because we know opportunity doesn't just fall into our laps. We clean your offices, build your homes, care for your children, and often, for your elders. We labour, we strive, we become part of the very fabric of this society. Yet, too often, we are met not with open arms, but with suspicion, with whispers, with outright hostility. It's in the sideways glances at the grocery store, the muttered comments about "taking our jobs," the landlords who refuse our applications, the jobs we're qualified for but never get. It's in the news headlines that paint us all with the same broad brush, labelling us as criminals or burdens, ignoring the substantial majority of us who are simply trying to build a better life.

The impact of this discrimination is far-reaching. It's not just hurt feelings. It chips away at our confidence, makes us question our worth. It makes us afraid, sometimes, to walk down the street, to speak our own languages, to simply exist. It makes it harder to find housing, to get a good education, to access healthcare. It makes it harder to climb the ladder, to achieve the dreams that brought us here in the first place. And for our children, the ones born here, the ones who speak your language fluently and pledge allegiance to your flag, the sting is perhaps even sharper. They are caught between two worlds, not fully belonging to either. They inherit the accent of their parents, the "otherness" that clings to them like a shadow, even when they've never set foot in the land of their ancestors. They face bullying in the schoolyard, micro-aggressions in the workplace, and the persistent pressure to prove their loyalty, to justify their presence. We are not asking for special treatment. We are simply asking for fairness, for respect, for the chance to employ our talents and our hard work without facing prejudice. We are asking to be seen not as "immigrants," but as individuals, as neighbours, as human beings. Because beneath the different languages, the different customs, the different skin colours, we all share the same fundamental desires: to provide for our families, to build a better future, and to live in peace and dignity. We are all, in the end, just people, trying to make a home in this world.

Discrimination and prejudice – they're not just words. They're a burden, an unceasing battle. But they also ignite a fire. A fire of determination to prove the stereotypes wrong, to rise above the negativity, to build a life filled with purpose and pride. Because we, the immigrants, are not defined by the prejudice we face. We are defined by our resolve, our strength, and our unshakeable faith in the possibility of a better future.

CHAPTER SIX

THE WORLD THEIR CAMPUS

Aisha moved from Nigeria to England to study. Everything was different. The quiet, well-stocked library in London was a world away from the sparsely equipped learning environment she knew before. Learning astrophysics in the academic setting was hard, like trying to catch slippery fish. She felt small and lost in this new place. Just months ago, Nigeria was her academic universe. Now, England, with its varied weather and unfamiliar customs, was her new cosmos, and she, a tiny speck, was trying to find her place within it. She represented one of the numerous individual contributions that constitute the wide structure of global education– an immigrant student. She, like many others drawn to foreign lands for academic pursuits, carried a suitcase not just of clothes, but of dreams, ambitions, and the expectations from families who had often sacrificed greatly for this opportunity. Her story, like theirs, was one of formidable challenges and hard-won successes, a tribute to the transformative power of education. The opening test, a monstrous wave crashing upon the shore of their new lives, was language. Even with prior English education, the patterns of classroom discourse, the slang swirling in student lounges, the quick-fire debates in seminars – it was all a bewildering symphony of unfamiliar sounds.

Kenji, a bright engineering student from Tokyo, found himself nodding politely in lectures in London, understanding the technical terms but missing the subtle jokes and cultural references that punctuated the professor's delivery. His carefully prepared presentations felt stilted and overly formal in a room buzzing with casual banter. "It's like trying to swim in treacle," he confessed to Aisha one evening, both of them seeking refuge in the international student common room. Beyond language, the cultural chasm yawned wide. What was considered polite discourse in one country could be perceived as aggressive in another. Classroom participation norms varied drastically.

Elena, a fiercely intelligent history student from Ukraine, accustomed to a more formal, teacher-centred approach, initially felt out of her depth in the collaborative, discussion-driven seminars in her Parisian university. Silence, in her culture, signified respect and contemplation. Here, it was often interpreted as disengagement. She learned to navigate the unspoken rules, to raise her hand at the right moment, to interject confidently, even when her palms were slick with nervousness.

The pedagogical approaches presented a disorienting array of enigmas. Assessment methods differed drastically. Students accustomed to rote learning might find themselves unprepared for critical thinking essays demanded in Western universities. Those used to structured curricula found the freedom and self-directed learning emphasized in some teaching philosophies both liberating and intimidating. The enormous volume of reading, the expectation of independent research, the sustained pressure to perform – it was a relentless academic marathon. Adding to the intellectual strain was the emotional toll of displacement. Homesickness was a companion, a quiet ache in the chest. The aroma of unfamiliar spices wafting from street vendors, the absence of familiar faces, the utter foreignness of everything – it could be isolating. For many, the financial burden was immense. Visa costs, tuition fees, living expenses in often expensive cities – the pressure to make ends meet often forced students into part-time jobs, adding another layer of exhaustion to their already demanding schedules. However, amidst these turbulent waters, islands of success emerged. Aisha, Kenji, Elena, and others like them, armed with their determination and intellect, began to build bridges across these divides. Language classes, often made available by the universities, were lifelines. International student societies became crucial support networks, spaces where shared experiences were validated, friendships forged, and cultural misunderstandings gently navigated. Mentors, both faculty and senior students, offered invaluable guidance, acting as compasses in the unfamiliar academic landscape. Slowly, painstakingly, these students started to thrive.

Kenji, previously hesitant, discovered the power of online language learning tools and embraced the informal learning opportunities of interacting with native English speakers in his lab. His presentations, while still carrying a touch of his characteristic formality, gained a confident edge.

Elena, by observing her peers and seeking feedback from her professors, learned to actively participate in seminars, her insightful contributions earning her the respect of her classmates.

Aisha, after weeks of feeling adrift in astrophysics, found a breakthrough when she joined a study group with other international students. Sharing their struggles, explaining concepts to each other in simpler terms, they unlocked the technicalities of the subject together. She discovered a hidden strength in her persistence, a newfound confidence in her ability to overcome obstacles.

Success for immigrant students was often an important and daring personal achievement. It wasn't always about topping the class, though many did achieve academic excellence. Success was about mastering a new language, not just for academic purposes but to truly connect with the people around them. It was about navigating a foreign culture, adapting to new norms while holding onto their own identities. It was about building a community far from home, finding belonging in a place that initially felt alien. It was about proving to themselves, and to their families who had invested so much in them, that they could not just survive, but flourish.

Years later, Aisha stood on the stage at her graduation ceremony in London, the autumn leaves swirling outside the grand hall. She looked out at the multitude of faces, a vibrant mix of nationalities, each with their own story of challenges overcome and dreams realised. She had not just learned astrophysics; she had learned adaptability and the interconnectedness of the world. She had built bridges with books, navigated rivers of resilience, and emerged not just as a graduate, but as a global citizen, ready to contribute her distinctive perspective and talents to a world increasingly enriched by the journeys of immigrant students. Her success, like that of thousands upon thousands of others who dared to cross borders for knowledge, was a clear demonstration of the enduring power of education to transcend boundaries and build a brighter, more interconnected future.

Navigating the Education System

Imagine stepping onto foreign soil, clutching not just a suitcase, but a future. For immigrant students, this isn't just a geographical relocation; it's a plunge into a new world, a sudden confrontation with a new education, culture, and language. They arrive with the layered stories of their homelands, not as blank slates, and they are rich with potential, yes, but also carrying the baggage of unspoken anxieties and the ghosts of cultures left behind. Their journey in a foreign educational system is gripping- a compelling drama of daunting mires met with breath-taking grit that dares to dream beyond borders.- Let's walk with them for a moment, feel the ground shift beneath their feet.

Picture the first lecture hall, the professor's rapid-fire delivery in a language still clinging to the edges of comprehension. Imagine the bewildered smile as they navigate social cues that are invisible to them, the awkward silences in group projects where cultural patterns clash. These are not minor inconveniences; they are daily skirmishes in a silent battle for belonging, for academic survival.

Immigrant students face several significant challenges. Language is the most immediate hobble. Academic language, with its sophisticated vocabulary and implicit assumptions, differs greatly from conversational fluency. This can lead to feelings of isolation and difficulty in fully participating in academic discussions and assignments.
Cultural differences also pose a major hurdle. Unspoken norms and expectations in the host country's educational system can be confusing and lead to misunderstandings. Students may have trouble adapting to different communication styles and social interactions, with repercussions for their social integration and sense of belonging.
Academic adjustment is another crux. Educational systems vary widely, and students may find they lack foundational knowledge in certain areas. This requires them to work harder to catch up to their peers, adding to their academic workload.
Social isolation is a common experience. Leaving behind familiar support strategies can lead to loneliness and difficulty forming new connections. Language barriers, cultural differences, and underlying biases can further hinder social integration.
Financial pressures are often substantial. International student fees, living expenses, and limited scholarship opportunities can create notable financial strain. Many students must balance

demanding coursework with part-time jobs, leading to increased stress and the need to make sacrifices. The cumulative effect of these can take a severe psychological and emotional toll. Culture shock, homesickness, and the pressure to succeed can lead to anxiety, depression, and feelings of inadequacy.

Despite these challenges, many immigrant students achieve remarkable academic success. Their diligence and appreciation for the opportunity often motivate them to excel. They develop valuable skills in cross-cultural communication and adaptation, becoming bridge-builders between cultures. Their presence enriches educational environments and promotes a more interconnected world. And the rewards extend far beyond the academic. Their international education becomes a launchpad to global careers. Bilingualism, intercultural competence, mettle – these are the currencies of the 21st-century job market. Imagine the doors that open to them, the global networks they build, the career paths that unfurl before them, all paved by the hard-won experiences of their immigrant journey. They become global citizens, equipped not just with degrees, but with the invaluable skillset to thrive in an interconnected world, ready to make their mark on a global stage. But their greatest triumph lies in their contribution to the very fabric of their host societies. They don't just receive an education; they enrich the educational landscape with their diverse lenses, their unique insights, and their tenacity. Imagine the vibrant energy they bring to classrooms, the fresh ideas they inject into research, the global interpretations they share in every discussion. They broaden horizons, provoke new thinking about assumptions, and foster a more inclusive, globally-minded environment for all. Their presence is not just a benefit; it's a cornerstone, a necessary spice that enriches the intellectual and cultural stew of their adopted homes. Theirs is a story that demands our attention, our understanding, and most importantly, our active support.

To truly unlock the extraordinary potential of immigrant students, we, as educators, as institutions, as societies, must become architects of welcome, builders of bridges, clearers of pathways. We must invest in robust language support, cultivate culturally responsive classrooms, build bridges to social integration, and dismantle financial obstacles. We must recognise the arduous emotional journey they undertake and implement accessible, culturally sensitive support mechanisms. For within the adversities and successes of immigrant students lies a powerful lesson: that crossing borders is not just about seeking a better life; it's about enriching the world with diverse perspectives and the enduring power of hope itself. Their stories are not just about individual triumphs; they are about building a more inclusive, interconnected, and vibrant future for us all.

Let us listen, let us learn, and let us actively participate in writing the next chapter of their extraordinary journey.

CHAPTER SEVEN

UNLOCKING POTENTIAL

They say opportunity awaits in new lands. They paint pictures of streets paved with gold, of meritocracies where hard work alone guarantees success. As immigrants, we come clutching those stories, fuelled by hope and a fierce willpower to build a better life. We arrive with our skills, our educations, our experiences, ready to contribute, eager to be a part to the formation of a new society. But the reality, the cold, hard reality, that slams into us often with the force of a brick wall, is the agonising, demoralising, and often discriminatory labyrinth of finding meaningful employment. It's a cruel irony, isn't it? We are welcomed, in a way. Our labour is desired, often in essential, yet undervalued sectors. We see the "Help Wanted" signs plastered everywhere, promising jobs. But the moment we step beyond those entry-level roles, the moment we aim for work that truly utilises our skills, our qualifications, the doors begin to narrow, the pathways become choked with obstacles.

Proving Who You Are All Over Again

Okay, let's just think about this for a second, shall we? You've actually done it. Years, I'm talking years of hitting the books, stressing over exams, practically living in the lab or studio or wherever it was you were perfecting your thing. You've sweated, you've pushed, you've honed your skills. And you know what? You earned that piece of paper. That engineering degree, that medical license, that project management certification – whatever it is, it's not just a flimsy document. It's concrete proof. It's a testament to your damn dedication, your intellect, the absolute force of your capabilities. So, picture this. You arrive, full of hope, maybe a little nervous, but excited for what's next. And then, boom. You get hit with it, the cold, hard truth. In essence, you're told, flat out, "Yeah, well, that doesn't really count here." Doesn't count? Are you kidding me? This, my friends, is the credential recognition conundrum. It's a soul-crushing, spirit-draining maze of pointless bureaucracy, a blatant devaluation of everything you've worked for, and frankly, it's utterly unbelievable.

Let me try to paint you a picture. Imagine you're dropped in the middle of a completely foreign city. No map. Okay, bad enough, right? But wait, there's more. The map you do find keeps changing on you, street names morphing, buildings vanishing, and all the signs. Forget about it. They're in some language you can barely decipher. That, in a nutshell, is what it feels like trying to get your hard-earned foreign qualifications recognised. You're thrown headfirst into a system where every single profession, every single industry, seems to have dreamt up its own ridiculous, completely arbitrary set of rules. And the million-dollar question? Who the heck do you even ask for help? Which forms? God, the forms! What hoops are you expected to jump through, and seriously, how long is this going to take? The whole damn process is deliberately shrouded in fog, thick as pea soup. It leaves immigrants feeling utterly, hopelessly lost. Like they're trapped in some kind of Kafkaesque nightmare where all their past achievements, all their skills, their very identities, are rendered invisible, meaningless in the eyes of their shiny new country.

And even if, by some pure stroke of luck, you actually get through, you won't believe what happens next! You're still not out of the woods. Devaluation could be waiting around the corner to smack you in the face. Imagine this – you carefully, meticulously craft a masterpiece. You pour every ounce of effort into it. And then you present it, brimming with pride, only to have someone glance at it dismissively and just shrug it off.

"Yeah, nice," they say, with this condescending tone, "but it's… foreign." That's the attitude.

Professions like law, which are jurisdiction-specific, require domestic study for licensure. Foreign law degrees are often not recognised. Even outside of regulated fields, international degrees from universities abroad, even freakin' renowned institutions, are often viewed with suspicion, treated as somehow inherently "lesser" than the ones churned out locally. Years of real-world experience, projects successfully completed, genuine achievements celebrated elsewhere – all of it can be casually discounted, deemed "not relevant" or, my personal favourite, "not up to our standards." It's a grave insult, a direct slap in the face. It's a denial of the very skills and expertise that an immigrant brings, forcing them to start from absolute scratch, often stuck in entry-level jobs that are frankly insulting considering their true potential. It's not just frustrating, you know? It's downright economically nonsensical. We are literally, actively, throwing away valuable talent. Letting crucial skills wither and die on the vine while we force perfectly capable immigrants to jump through these completely needless, ridiculously expensive, and utterly demoralising hoops.

Then, just to add insult to injury, there's the financial burden. The seriously hefty price tag attached to simply proving who you are, what you know. Recertification, these so-called "bridging programs," licensing exams – often mandatory, always expensive. And they hit you precisely when you are at your most financially vulnerable. Freshly relocated, facing all the insane costs that come with it, often with savings completely depleted. It's a system that feels rigged, designed to bleed you dry, demanding immigrants pay again and again and again to demonstrate skills they already bloody well possess. Skills that their home countries have already, very thoroughly, validated. And time? Don't even get me started on the time. Years, I tell you, years can be lost just navigating these utterly pointless processes. Years that could be spent working, contributing to society, building a future, a life. Instead? They're caught in this ridiculous holding pattern, their professional lives frozen solid, their dreams put on indefinite hold, and their pockets slowly, agonisingly, emptying.

Oh, and let's not for a single second forget the ever-present, always looming phantom of language proficiency. It is weaponized, plain and simple, used as a convenient, socially acceptable pretext. Of course, communication is key, I'm not arguing with that. But for immigrants, language proficiency too often becomes a moving target, a standard deliberately raised to be impossibly high, cynically used as a convenient excuse to deny recognition even when their communication skills are perfectly, demonstrably, adequate for the job. Think about it. Imagine you're a brilliant surgeon. Fluent in all the medical terminology, capable of performing life-saving procedures with your eyes closed. And then you're told, with a straight face, that your accent is "too strong" to actually practice in your field. Seriously? It's not about competence, people. It's prejudice, pure and simple, dressed up and disguised as a language requirement. And it stinks.

Loss for All of Us

The consequences of these barriers ripple outwards, affecting not just individual immigrants, but our entire societies. Imagine a symphony orchestra with half its musicians silenced, their instruments gathering dust. That's the sound of untapped immigrant potential, the music we're all missing out on.

For immigrants, the cost is devastating. Underemployment and deskilling become a soul-crushing reality. Doctors driving taxis, engineers working as delivery drivers – these are not just anecdotal stories; they are symptoms of a system failing to utilise valuable talent. Financial hardship becomes a serious ordeal, pushing families into poverty, thereby undermining the very economic security they sought. And the psychological toll is immense – the frustration, the anxiety, the erosion of self-worth, the pervasive sense of injustice. Dreams deferred, potential wasted, lives diminished. But the loss isn't just theirs; it's ours too. We suffer economic losses when we underutilise immigrant skills. Innovation stagnates, productivity suffers, and economic growth is stunted. We create social inequalities when we routinely marginalise a large portion of our population, undermining social cohesion and eroding trust. And we simply miss out on the vibrant diversity immigrants represent – a wealth of varied thought, innovative ideas, cultural capital that could enrich our workplaces, our communities, our entire nations.

The untapped potential of immigrants is a boundless and precious resource. It's time to stop locking it away behind walls of bureaucracy and prejudice. It's time to unlock that potential, to create a framework where skills are valued, talent is recognised, and everyone, regardless of their origin, has the opportunity to contribute, to thrive, and to build a better future – for themselves, and for all of us. It's not just the right thing to do; it's the smart thing to do. Let's start building those bridges, tearing down those walls, and finally unleash the power of immigrant talent to enrich and strengthen our world.

CHAPTER EIGHT

BUILDING A NEW LIFE

S even thousand miles. That's how far I was from Ateseme and my boys, Jayden and Gearld. Seven thousand miles of ocean and a mountain of financial pressure. The humid air of Lagos clung to my memory, a world away from the sharp, biting wind that now whipped at my face in London. They called it the land of opportunity. But all I felt was the gnawing emptiness in my pockets and the tightening knot of worry in my stomach. For the past six months, opportunity had felt more like a mirage shimmering on the horizon.

Back home, I had a career, respect. Here, I was anonymous, just another immigrant in a sea of faces. My qualifications, once a source of pride, were worthless in this city. My CV joined scores of others, discarded and forgotten. The doors were closed, the accents impenetrable, and my past achievements seemed to count for absolutely nothing. The initial excitement of arriving had quickly faded, replaced by the harsh reality of survival. The cramped room I shared with three other men swallowed a huge chunk of my meagre savings. The rent was exorbitant, pressing down on me. Food, transportation, even the simplest necessities – they all cost more than I'd anticipated. I'd taken any job I could find. Cleaning offices at night, delivering takeaways in the freezing rain, even working construction, my hands calloused and aching. It was honest work, and I was grateful for it, but the pay was barely enough to cover the essentials. And it wasn't what I came here for. I came to build a better life, not just scrape by.

The pressure was immense. Ateseme, my wife, and our two children were still in Lagos, relying on the money I sent home. Every pound I spent here was a pound less for them. I could picture her face, etched with worry, and my children's, their eyes full of hope for a future I was struggling to provide. Sometimes, standing on the deserted streets at 3 am, the city lights blurring through the rain, I would feel a wave of despair wash over me. Had I made the right decision? Had I traded one set of problems for another? The gnawing loneliness, the worry that wouldn't stop, the sheer difficulty of it all... it was almost enough to break me. Guilt was my shadow. I felt like I was failing them, failing myself. I'd promised them a better life, but all I seemed to be doing was sinking deeper into debt and despair.

The phone calls home were bittersweet. She would tell me about the children's progress in school, about her dreams for their future, and I'd force a smile, pretending that everything was going according to plan. Sleep offered little respite. I'd lie awake at night, the hum of the city reverberating as my thoughts churned with my plight. I'd calculate and recalculate our finances, trying to make the numbers work, but they never did. The anxiety was a physical thing, a tightness in my chest, a nagging knot in my stomach.

But then I would think of Ateseme - my Sunshine, of Jayden and Gerald, their faces etched in my memory. They would reignite my purpose. I had to keep going. I had to keep pushing. The dream, even if it was a distant glimmer, was all I had. It was the fuel that kept me going, the hope that one day, I would bring my family here, to this land of supposed opportunity, and together, we would build a better life, a life where the dream wasn't just a whisper in the wind, but a tangible reality. I knew I wasn't alone. I'd met other immigrants, men and women with similar stories, similar struggles. We'd share our experiences, our frustrations, our hopes. We'd offer each other what little support we could, a shared meal, a word of encouragement. We were all in the same boat, navigating the choppy waters of a new life, clinging to the hope that things would eventually get better.

In the course of time, I happened upon an advertisement for a skills training program specifically designed for IT professionals. It was a long shot, and it would cost money I didn't have, but it was a chance, a glimmer of hope in the darkness. I decided to apply. I had nothing to lose.

The financial pressures of being an immigrant were immense, like a tidal wave that threatened to pull me under. But I refused to give up. I had a family to support, a dream to chase. And I knew that even in the face of formidable odds, hope, like the Lagos sun, could still rise and illuminate the path forward. It might be a long and arduous journey, but I would keep walking, one step at a time, one day at a time, until I reached the other side.

The Cost of a New Beginning

Let's dispel a myth right away: new beginnings aren't free. They come with a price tag, often invisible at first glance, yet etched indelibly into the lives of those who dare to chase them. For immigrants, this price is particularly steep, an extensive calculus of sacrifices and losses often overshadowed by the dazzling promise of a brighter future. We celebrate the stories of triumph, the recuperation, the rebuilding – and rightfully so. But to truly understand the immigrant experience, we must also confront the profound costs, the hidden ledger of loss that accompanies the leap of faith into a new world.

Imagine packing your life into a suitcase, or maybe two. Not just clothes and trinkets, but memories, traditions, a lifetime of familiar comforts condensed into something portable. What gets left behind is not just stuff; it's a piece of your soul. This is the first down payment on a new beginning – the tangible financial cost. Moving across borders isn't cheap. There are visa fees, travel expenses, the exorbitant cost of setting up a new home from scratch. Savings accounts are drained, families mortgage their futures, just to afford the ticket to hope. Then comes the daily grind – higher rents in unfamiliar cities, the cost of living in a place where you haven't yet established yourself, haven't built a safety net. The early days are often a tightrope walk of financial precarity, every penny scrutinised, every expense weighed against the dream. This isn't just about budgeting; it's about an ongoing, low-hum anxiety that vibrates beneath the surface of daily life, a fear that one unexpected bill could unravel everything.

But the ledger of loss for immigrants extends far beyond the purely financial. Consider the emotional cost, a weight that settles onto shoulders often unseen. Leaving home is a form of grief, a severance from the familiar comfort of culture, language, and ingrained social cadence. It's saying goodbye to the scent of your grandmother's kitchen, the easy banter of your native tongue filling the local market, the comforting predictability of traditions reflecting through your year. These aren't just quaint details; they are the strands of identity, the anchors of belonging. In their absence, a void opens up, a space filled with homesickness, a yearning for a past that can never be fully replicated. Imagine trying to explain inside jokes in a new language, to share cultural references that land with a thudding silence, to feel like a muted version of yourself in conversations, constantly editing, explaining, translating not just words, but entire ways of being. This unbroken negotiation of identity, this daily dance between two worlds, is emotionally exhausting, a quiet toll taken on the psyche.

Then there's the social cost, the dismantling and rebuilding of a life's intricate network. For many, immigration means leaving behind a lifetime of relationships – family, friends, community, the very fabric of social support that we all rely on. Imagine arriving in a new place, feeling like a lone ship on a vast ocean, surrounded by unfamiliar faces, the chatter of unknown voices. Building new connections takes time, vulnerability, and often, the navigation of cultural worlds. Especially in the early days, loneliness is often felt as a gnawing emptiness that amplifies the stress of all other glitches. It's not just about missing people; it's about losing the effortless ease of understanding, of being understood, of sharing a common frame of reference, of having a readily available safety net of familiar faces in times of need. This social re-wiring, this deliberate construction of a new community from scratch, demands immense emotional energy and toughness.

And let's not overlook the professional cost, often a bitter pill for skilled immigrants to swallow. Imagine holding a prestigious degree from your home country, years of experience under your belt, only to find that your qualifications are met with scepticism, devaluation, or outright dismissal in your new land. The arduous process of credential recognition, the often-discriminatory practices in hiring, the subtle biases that favour "local" experience – these create substantial hindrances to meaningful employment. Skilled immigrants often find themselves underemployed, taking jobs far below their skill level, their talents and expertise tragically wasted. It's a demoralising experience, an uphill battle to prove their worth, to be seen for their abilities rather than their origins. This professional limbo not only impacts financial stability but also erodes self-esteem and purpose, adding another layer of emotional trauma to an already heavy burden.

Perhaps the most insidious cost is the psychological toll, the unseen wear and tear on mental wellbeing. Imagine living with perpetual uncertainty, navigating the arduous immigration systems, dealing with culture shock, facing the risk of discrimination, alongside financial anxieties and social isolation. The prolonged stress, the relentless pressure to succeed, to integrate, to justify the enormous leap of faith-these factors severely impact mental health. Anxiety becomes a pervasive undercurrent, depression a shadow lurking in the corners, and feelings of inadequacy can chip away at self-worth. The immigrant journey, while filled with potential rewards, is also inherently traumatic, a process of displacement, assimilation, and non-stop negotiation with the unfamiliar. Yet, mental health support for immigrants is often under-resourced, inaccessible, or culturally insensitive, leaving many to navigate these psychological predicaments alone, further compounding their vulnerability.

And finally, there's the cost of time, an often-overlooked element. Immigration is not a sprint; it's a marathon, often run uphill in shifting sands. Years can be spent navigating bureaucratic processes, waiting for decisions, rebuilding careers, learning new languages, and establishing belonging. These are not overnight transformations; they are gradual, incremental processes demanding patience, perseverance, and a willingness to endure prolonged periods of uncertainty and instability. This time cost represents a weighty investment, a portion of life surrendered to the demands of building a new beginning, time that could have been spent in more settled, comfortable circumstances, time that is irrevocably lost from the past and dedicated to a future still uncertain.

The cost of a new beginning for immigrants is not a simple sum; it's a difficult equation with variables that are both tangible and intimately personal. It is an inventory of financial sacrifices, emotional losses, social upheavals, professional setbacks, psychological burdens, and the relentless investment of time. Understanding these hidden costs is not to diminish the hope and what can be achieved through immigration, but to truly appreciate the depth of courage and sheer grit required to embark on this transformative journey. It's about recognising the price tag attached to hope, acknowledging the true depth of sacrifices made in pursuit of a better future, and fostering societies that are not only welcoming but also genuinely supportive, ensuring that the promise of a new beginning is not just a dream, but a tangible reality accessible to all who dare to seek it.

The Pursuit of the American Dream

The American Dream, that potent and perpetually evolving promise of upward mobility, prosperity, and freedom, has been a siren song attracting generations to the shores of the United States. But for no group is this pursuit more fraught, more keenly felt, and ultimately more transformative than for immigrants. Their journey to and within America is not merely a quest for individual betterment, but an engagement that goes to the very heart of the Dream itself, often revealing its shimmering bright side alongside its stark, unyielding realities.

For immigrants, the American Dream often begins as a guiding thought across oceans and borders. Fuelled by narratives of streets paved with gold and opportunities abundant for the taking, they are propelled by a potent mix of hope and desperation. Often leaving behind hardship – poverty, political instability, persecution, or simply a perceived lack of prospects – the Dream represents a radical departure from the constraints of their past. It is a promise of agency, of personal autonomy, where hard work and meritocracy are supposed to be the keys to unlocking a better life, not just for themselves, but often, sacrificially, for their families. This preceding vision is often idealised, a romanticised notion gleaned from stories, films, and whispered promises. It's a Dream painted in broad strokes of economic security, educational advancement, and personal liberty. However, the immigrant experience quickly confronts this idealised image with the shades and often harsh realities of American life. The "pursuit" swiftly transforms from a hopeful imagining into a relentless uphill climb. Language barriers, cultural adjustments, and the transition to a new system become immediate hurdles. The gold-paved streets often turn out to be potholed and uneven, demanding not just hard work, but also stamina, flexibility, and a thick skin. Discrimination, both overt and institutionally embedded, becomes a tangible barrier, challenging the very notion of meritocracy that underpins the Dream. Immigrants often find themselves in precarious economic situations, taking on demanding jobs that native-born citizens might eschew, struggling to make ends meet while navigating unfamiliar social landscapes.

Yet, despite these formidable setbacks, the immigrant pursuit of the American Dream often possesses a unique intensity and clarity. Having consciously chosen to leave behind their homeland, immigrants bring with them a level of commitment that does not falter and a genuine appreciation for the opportunities, however imperfect, that America offers. They frequently exhibit a remarkable work ethic, a willingness to sacrifice, and a deep-seated belief in education as a pathway to advancement. Their struggles, rather than diminishing the Dream, often sharpen their understanding of its core tenets. For many, the Dream shifts from opulent wealth to something more foundational: stability, security for their children, the freedom to practice their culture and religion, and the chance to contribute to their new society.

Notably, the immigrant experience also redefines and enriches the American Dream itself. Immigrants don't just passively assimilate; they are active in the cultural, economic, and social landscape of America. They bring with them diverse skills, fresh outlooks, and entrepreneurial spirits, invigorating industries and communities. They challenge the prevailing ideas and broaden the definition of success. Their stories become integral to the evolving narrative of the Dream, reminding America of its foundational promise as a nation built by and for immigrants.

However, it's imperative to acknowledge that the immigrant experience is not monolithic. The Dream's accessibility is hugely impacted by factors like race, class, legal status, and country of origin. For some immigrant groups, particularly those facing racial discrimination and restrictive immigration policies, the pursuit can feel perpetually elusive, the Dream receding further into the distance with each generation. The promise of equality and opportunity can feel hollow when confronted with entrenched inequalities and prejudice. This reality necessitates a critical examination of the American Dream – is it truly accessible to all, or are there inherent impediments that limit its reach for certain groups, particularly those who are marginalised and vulnerable?

The immigrant experience unveils a powerful and illuminating lens through which to understand the American Dream. It is a pursuit fuelled by hope and tenacity, often born from necessity and shaped by hardship. While the idealised Dream might clash with the realities of integration and societal frictions, the immigrant journey ultimately underscores the Dream's enduring allure and its capacity for revolution and redefinition. It compels us to ask critical questions about the Dream's inclusivity and accessibility, while simultaneously celebrating the invaluable contributions and the spirit of perseverance of those who continue to chase its shimmering promise, enriching America as they concretely pursue it.

The story of the American Dream, therefore, is inextricably intertwined with the story of the immigrant, a narrative still being written, shaped by both the glittering promises and the unvarnished truths of life in the land of opportunity.

Beyond American Borders, a Universal Yearning

The "American Dream" – the very phrase conjures images of sprawling suburbs, picket fences, and opportunities blossoming like fields of wheat under a boundless sky. It's a concept inextricably linked to the United States; a nation literally forged in the crucible of immigration. From the Pilgrims seeking religious freedom to waves of newcomers chasing economic prosperity, America has long been perceived as the land where hard work and determination could pave the road to a brighter future. This narrative, firmly embedded in the national identity, is not just a historical artifact; it continues to fuel aspirations and draw individuals from every corner of the globe. But to confine the dream of a better life to solely American shores is to misunderstand its fundamental nature.

For immigrants, the yearning for a brighter future isn't defined by geographical coordinates; it's a core human impulse, a universal quest that transcends national flags and borderlines. The motivations for individuals to leave their homes, families, and familiar landscapes are often rooted in a fundamental desire for betterment – for safety, for opportunity, for a life unburdened by hardship. Whether they are drawn to the promise of the "American Dream," the allure of European stability, the burgeoning economies of Asia, or the developing landscapes of Africa, immigrants are impelled by a common phenomenon: the desire for a life that offers more than their present circumstances. This "more" can take many forms – economic stability, access to quality education and healthcare, freedom from persecution or conflict, or simply the chance to build a life of dignity and purpose. These are not uniquely "American" desires; they are aspirations that resonate infinitely within us all across cultures and continents. The "American Dream," in its idealised form, speaks to these universal longings – the promise of upward mobility, the belief in self-reliance, and the opportunity to create a better life for oneself and future generations. This is precisely why it has resonated so powerfully across the globe, becoming a shorthand for hope and possibility. However, the essence of the dream isn't tied to a specific nationality. It's about the fundamental immanent urge to strive, to improve, and to seek a future that shines brighter than the past.

Therefore, while the "American Dream" is undeniably a product of the United States and its history of immigration, it serves as a powerful symbol for a much larger, more universal human narrative. It's the story of steadfastness, courage, and the abiding hope that a better life is attainable, no matter where one chooses to plant their roots. For immigrants everywhere, the dream of a better life is not defined by a single nation, but by the boundless capacity of the psyche to seek, to hope, and to build a brighter future, wherever it may be found.

CHAPTER NINE

WEAVING NEW TIES

S ulaiman Yusufu's dreams of London had collided with a harsh reality. The city, imposing and grey, held none of the warmth he'd left behind in Lagos. The rain hammering against his window brought back his disappointment. He had come seeking opportunity, but found only a cold indifference, a vastness that swallowed him whole. Back home, family was everything: his wife, Tinuade, her laughter like music, a melody that lifted the spirits; his three children, their energy filling their small apartment; his mother's prayers; his father's wise counsel. They were a unit, inseparable by love and shared experiences. Here, Sulaiman was just one man, a face in a sea of faces.

His first few weeks were a blur. The tiny, cramped room he rented, the endless job applications that went unanswered, the bewildering Tube railways. He missed the familiar smells of suya and jollof rice, the sound of Yoruba being spoken on the streets, the warmth of human connection. He'd call Tinuade, the line crackling, her voice a lifeline. He'd paint a picture of London life, trying to sound positive, but the truth was, he was struggling.

One Sunday, Sulaiman decided to visit a Nigerian restaurant he'd found online. The aroma of pounded yam and egusi soup hit him like a punch to the gut, a wave of nostalgia so strong it almost brought tears to his eyes. As he ate, he overheard a conversation in Yoruba. He turned and saw a group of men, laughing and talking, their faces familiar, welcoming. He hesitated, then walked over.

"Excuse me," he said, in Yoruba. "Are you... are you from Nigeria?"

Their faces lit up.

"Ah, brother!" one of them exclaimed.

"Welcome! Come, sit with us."

That chance encounter changed everything. They were members of a Nigerian community association, a group of men who met regularly to share stories, offer support, and celebrate their culture. They'd all been through the same struggles – the loneliness, the job hunting, the cultural adjustments. They told Sulaiman about job opportunities, introduced him to other Nigerians in the city, even helped him find his way through the challenging housing arrangements. They became his family away from family. They celebrated birthdays, shared meals, and watched football together. They taught him where to find African ingredients, where to get his hair braided, where to send money home. Through them, Sulaiman wasn't just a stranger in a strange land anymore. He was part of a community, bound by shared heritage and a common experience. The loneliness began to recede, and in its place, connection and support blossomed.

Eventually, Sulaiman found a decent job, moved to a slightly bigger flat, and saved enough money to bring Tinuade and the children over. The reunion at Heathrow was joyous, tears flowing freely. They were together again, their little family unit complete. London still presented its difficulties, but with the support of his newfound community, it became bearable, even enjoyable. Sulaiman learned that family isn't just about blood. It's about connection, about shared experiences, about the unwavering support you find when you're far from home.

In that cold, bustling city, he discovered the true meaning of community, the bond of shared heritage, and the power of human connection to make a foreign land feel like home. It wasn't Lagos, but it was their London, built on a foundation of love and the dependable support of a family forged in exile.

The Importance of Family

Consider yourself like a tree, abruptly relocated to a new and challenging environment. You're surrounded by unfamiliar sights, sounds, and customs. It can be an intimidating experience, a bit like being lost in a trackless, unknown forest. In this unfamiliar terrain, family can be your guiding stars, your compass, and your lifeline. They're the familiar faces that can ease your transition, the comforting voices that can dispel your fears, and the helping hands that can guide you through whatever comes your way.

Family support networks provide a decisive sense of belonging and stability in a foreign land. Family members understand the unique adjustments required for life in a new environment, offering empathy and encouragement that can be hard to find elsewhere.
Practical support is another invaluable aspect of family networks. From contending with regulatory red tape to finding suitable housing or schools, family members can pool their resources and knowledge to ease the transition. They can offer advice on local customs, translate documents, or simply lend a helping hand with everyday tasks. This practical assistance can alleviate much of the stress and allow newcomers to focus on settling in. Beyond the practicalities, family networks provide emotional sustenance. They offer an awareness of continuity and connection to one's roots, preserving cultural heritage and traditions. Sharing stories,

celebrating familiar holidays, and speaking one's native language within the family circle can be a powerful antidote to homesickness and cultural alienation.

Moreover, family support can play a pivotal role in mental well-being. The stress of adapting to a new culture can take a toll on one's mental health, leading to feelings of anxiety, isolation, or depression. Having a strong family network can buffer these effects, providing a safe space to express emotions, share concerns, and receive support.

Family support networks are an invaluable asset for those living in a foreign land. They provide practical assistance and emotional support, easing the rigours of cultural adjustment and fostering a smoother transition.

Whether it's immediate family or a wider network of relatives and close friends, these connections offer an indispensable lifeline, helping individuals establish themselves despite the tussle of life abroad while maintaining a strong hold on their identity and well-being.

The Potential for Exploitation

Family support can be a lifeline for immigrants, providing emotional, financial, and practical assistance during a challenging transition. However, it's important to be aware of the potential for exploitation. While most families are supportive and have the best intentions, some may take advantage of an immigrant's vulnerable position. This exploitation can take many forms. Some family members may ask for large sums of money, knowing that the immigrant may feel obligated to help. Others may take advantage of their knowledge of how things work, proposing help with paperwork or legal matters in exchange for favours or money. In some cases, family members may even try to control the immigrant's life, limiting their freedom and independence.

Blood and Burden

A rich, spicy aroma permeated the air, enveloping me in a comforting embrace against the cool October night. Friday, a wiry man with kind eyes and a hesitant smile, stirred the fragrant stew bubbling on his stove. I sat across from him in his tiny apartment, a space he'd managed to make feel like home with vibrant wall hangings and photographs of smiling faces.

"It smells wonderful, Friday," I said, genuinely impressed.

He chuckled, a low rumble in his chest. "My mother's recipe. It reminds me of home."

Home. A word packed with so many memories and sensations, I realised. For Friday, it was Nigeria. For me, it was this historic city. We'd met at the English language class I volunteered at. He'd been in the country for just over a year, and I'd been helping him sail through the often-confusing and unwieldy bureaucracy.

"How are things going?" I asked, careful to keep my tone casual. I knew he was working two jobs, a gruelling schedule that left him exhausted.

He sighed, the smile fading.

"Tough. Very tough. The money... it's never enough. I send most of it home, to my family."

He explained how his younger siblings were relying on him for school fees and his parents for medical expenses. It was a heavy burden, but he carried it with a quiet resolve.

"They need me," he said, his voice firm.

"Family is so important," I agreed, thinking of my own close-knit family. "They're lucky to have you, Friday."

"But..." He hesitated, stirring the stew a little too vigorously. "Sometimes... sometimes I wonder."

"Wonder what?" I prompted gently.

He looked up, his eyes meeting mine.

"My cousin, he helped me come here. He said he would find me work, a good place to live. He did, in a way. But... I pay him a lot of money every month. He says it's for helping me, for connecting me with people. But….." He trailed off, his unease palpable.

"But you're not sure?" I finished for him.

He nodded slowly. "The work… it's okay. But the rent he charges me… it's much more than what others pay for similar places. And the 'fees'… I don't understand them. He says it's how things work here."

My insides twisted with apprehension. I'd heard stories like this before. Immigrants, desperate to help their families, vulnerable and trusting, sometimes found themselves in exploitative situations.

"Friday," I said carefully, "I understand you want to support your family, and that your cousin helped you get started. That's wonderful. But it's also important to be sure you're not being taken advantage of. Do you have any paperwork for these payments you're making? Have you compared rent prices in this area?"

He looked down, shame flickering across his face. "No. I… I trust him. He's family."

"I understand that trust, Friday," I said softly. "But sometimes, even family can make mistakes. It's important to be informed. Maybe we could look at some rental listings together? And perhaps talk to someone at the Citizens Advice Bureau? They can give free, confidential advice about your rights."

He looked up, a glimmer of hope in his eyes.

"You would do that for me?"

I smiled. "Of course, Friday. Family support is a lifeline, but it shouldn't come at the cost of your own well-being. Let's make sure you're getting the support you need, and that you're not being exploited."

He nodded, a weight seeming to lift from his shoulders. The aroma of the stew, now mingled with the scent of hope, filled the small apartment. It was a long road ahead, but for the first time since he'd arrived, Friday wasn't walking it alone.

It's important for immigrants to be aware of these risks and to take steps to protect themselves. This might include setting clear boundaries with family members, seeking advice from trusted friends or community organisations, and documenting all financial transactions. Remember, it's okay to say no to family members if you feel uncomfortable or pressured.

The Importance of Community

The initial experience of immigrating is often one of profound disorientation. The unfamiliar language, customs, and social norms can leave you feeling adrift and isolated. It's in these moments that the true value of community becomes clear. For immigrants, community is more than just support; it's a vital connection. In those early days, community becomes your family away from family. It's the friendly face at the grocery store who speaks your language, the neighbour who is there to help you navigate the public transport, the cultural centre that hosts events celebrating your traditions. These seemingly small acts of kindness can make a world of difference when you're feeling isolated and disoriented.

Community is where you find connection. It's sharing stories with others who understand your journey, who know what it's like to leave everything behind and start anew. You can swap tips on everything from finding a good doctor to navigating the immigration process. You can celebrate holidays together, sharing traditional foods and laughter, keeping your culture alive in a new land.

Community is also a pillar of stability and support. When you're facing tough times – whether it's discrimination in the workplace or difficulty understanding a legal document – your community is there to offer advice, encouragement, and practical assistance.

They can connect you with resources, advocate for your rights, and help you acclimatise to your new life. Knowing you're not alone can make even the most unnerving obstacles feel surmountable. Beyond practical support, community provides something even more: a place where you can be yourself, where you're accepted for who you are, where your cultural background is valued and celebrated. It's a place where you can feel at home, even when you're thousands of miles away from your original one.

For me, and for so many other immigrants, community has been essential to our survival and our success. It's the anchor that keeps us grounded, the support that helps us thrive, and the bridge that connects us to our new home. It's where we find our voice, our sinew, and our place in the world. It's where we build our new lives, together.

The Intersection of Family and Community

For many of us immigrants, the journey to a new country isn't a solitary one. It's a family affair. We come seeking a better future, not just for ourselves, but for our children, our parents, our entire families. And intertwined with that family unit is the vital role of community. They become our lifeline, our anchor in a sea of unfamiliarity.

Family is the bedrock. It's the reason we take the leap, our firepower, and the ultimate measure of our success. We uproot our lives, leaving behind familiar surroundings, support systems, and often, even extended family, all for the hope of a brighter future for those we love. We carry their dreams on our shoulders, and their well-being becomes our primary focus. We navigate new terrains, learn new languages, and overcome myriad obstacles, all motivated by the desire to provide for our families and create opportunities they wouldn't have had back home.

Family is more than just those within our four walls; it extends to the wider immigrant community. We find ourselves drawn to others who share our experiences, who understand the challenges we face, and who speak our language – both literally and figuratively.

Community is where we find connection, in the shared laughter over communal meals, the comfort of speaking our mother tongue, and working together to navigate bureaucratic hurdles. It's where we celebrate our traditions, share our stories, and keep our cultures alive. It's where we find solace in knowing we're not alone. When we're far from home, these communities become our home away from home. Beyond emotional and cultural support, communities are also vital for practical assistance. From navigating the job market to understanding the school system, community members often become mentors, advisors, and advocates. They share resources, arrange childcare, and serve as a reservoir of support that can be crucial for successful integration. They help us understand the unspoken rules, the cultural differences, and the often-confusing conventions of our new country.

The intersection of family and community is where the immigrant experience truly comes to life. Family provides the motivation, the impetus, and the firm belief in a better future. Community provides the support, the connection, and the collective strength to make that future a reality. Together, they form the foundation upon which we build our new lives, our new identities, and our new homes. They are the crux of the immigrant story, evidence of the power of human connection in the face of immense change.

CHAPTER TEN

THE STRESS OF CHANGE

O n a quiet side street in the heart of London, far from the madding crowd, stood Habesha, a small Ethiopian café promising respite and authentic flavours. Its warm, earthy tones and the aroma of freshly brewed coffee proffered a momentary escape from the city's frenzy, a refuge for those seeking solace and a taste of home. Inside, Adina sat at a corner table, her gaze lost in the swirling patterns of her coffee cup. Her mind wandered back to the sun-kissed hills of her homeland, to the familiar laughter of her family, and the comforting flow of her old life. Leaving Ethiopia had been her choice, a pursuit of better opportunities, yet the pangs of homesickness often crept in, reminding her of the sacrifices she had made.

Across the table sat Kwame, a Ghanaian immigrant who had called London home for over a decade. His journey had been different, a forced departure from a country embroiled in political turmoil. The preceding years had been a blur of disorientation and loneliness, the weight of displacement pressing heavily on his soul. Yet, with time, he had found his footing, building a new community, a new life, layer by layer.

Their stories intertwined, a shared experience of cultural displacement. They spoke of the initial shock of encountering unfamiliar customs, the effort to learn a new language, and the yearning for the familiar comforts of home. They mourned the loss of their former identities, the ease with which they had moved through their native societies, now replaced by their status as perpetual outsiders. Yet, their stories resonated with the intrinsic capacity to adapt and find new connections. They spoke of the kindness of strangers, the unexpected friendships forged in shared adversity, and the slow, gradual process of building themselves anew. They discovered that home was not merely a physical place but a state of mind, a feeling that could be rekindled even in the most foreign of lands.

As the sun dipped below the London skyline, casting long shadows across the city, Adina and Kwame raised their cups in a silent toast—to the loved ones left behind, to the cultures that shaped them, and to the uncertain yet hopeful paths that lay ahead. Their stories echoed the experiences of generations of others, a reflection of the emotional toll of leaving loved ones and the enduring puissance of the psyche in the face of cultural displacement.

Leaving Loved Ones

Leaving loved ones behind – it's a wound that never fully heals. It's a dull throb that accompanies every joy and every challenge in this new land. You carry their faces with you, etched in your memory, their voices echoing within you. They're your touchstone, your connection to the life you left behind. It's not just the immediate family, though the pain of separation from parents, siblings, and children can feel unbearable at times. It's the extended family too – the grandparents who shared stories on warm evenings, the cousins you grew up with, the friends who were your loyal companions. These connections, which were once an integral part of your life back home, suddenly feel distant, fragile. You try to bridge the gap with phone calls and video chats, but it's never quite the same. The laughter feels a little muted, the shared jokes lose some of their flavour. You miss the casual intimacy, the unspoken understanding that comes from years of shared experiences. You miss the physical presence, the comfort of a hug, the simple joy of being together.

And then there's the guilt. The guilt of leaving them behind, of pursuing your own dreams while they remain in a place that may be struggling. The guilt of missing birthdays, holidays, and milestones. The guilt of not being there when they need you most. It's a heavy burden to carry, this guilt, and it often accompanies the immigrant journey. But amidst the pain and the guilt, there's also hope. Hope that one day, you'll be reunited. Hope that your sacrifices will create a better future for them too. Hope that the distance between you will eventually shrink. This hope is what sustains you, what keeps you going through the difficult times.

Leaving loved ones is perhaps the hardest part of the immigrant experience. It's a sacrifice, a heartbreaking loss that shapes every aspect of your new life. But it's also a testament to the strength of family bonds, a beacon of the love that transcends borders and oceans. It's a bittersweet symphony of longing and hope, a steady reminder of where you came from, and what you're working towards.

A Journey Through Shifting Identities

Jamila, a 22-year-old Eritrean immigrant, arrives in Berlin Germany, seeking a better life. Eager to assimilate, she embraces the new culture, adopting its language, fashion, and even dating customs. However, this rapid transformation alienates her from her family and community, who adhere to traditional values and customs. The young lady began to experience intense cultural displacement, feeling like an outsider in both her old and new worlds. The pressure to succeed in her new environment clashes with the expectations and traditions of her family, leading to frequent arguments and misunderstandings. She grappled with her identity, questioning her values and beliefs. She felt torn between honouring her heritage and embracing her new reality. The internal conflict bred debilitating self-doubt and a crippling detachment.

A turning point came with an encounter with someone who had walked a similar path. Jamila began to understand that she does not have to choose between the two cultures. She can find a way to bridge the gap, to honour her roots while embracing her new life. She started to reconnect with her heritage, find a community within the immigrant diaspora, and learned to communicate more effectively with her family. This journey of self-discovery led to newfound self-acceptance and belonging. Jamila found some measure of peace, accepting the full breadth of her identity. Though she sometimes feels displaced, she has come to appreciate and integrate her diverse cultural background.

The impact of leaving home creates a void that extends beyond the physical separation. It's the enduring cultural displacement, the lingering feeling of being slightly out of place. It's like walking through a city where you understand most of the words, but not the underlying rhythm of the conversation. You miss the familiar smells of your childhood kitchen, the way your neighbours used to chat on the street, the easy understanding that came with shared history and unspoken cues. Here, even simple things can feel complicated. A trip to the grocery store becomes a navigation exercise, deciphering unfamiliar brands and labels. A casual conversation can be fraught with occasional misunderstandings. You learn to reorient, to translate not just languages, but also cultural expressions, an often-exhausting process. It's not just the big things, like holidays and traditions, that you miss. It's the small things, the everyday rituals that gave your life its shape and meaning. The way your family used to gather for meals, the jokes you shared with your friends, the songs you used to sing – these are the pieces of your identity that feel displaced, like they pertain to a different time and place.

And then there's the dilemma of holding onto your own culture while trying to integrate into a new one. You want to honour your heritage, to pass it on to your children, but you also want them to feel that this is their place here, in this new country. It's a delicate balancing act, trying to preserve your roots while planting new ones. Sometimes you feel like you're living in two worlds, never fully fitting in either. Cultural displacement isn't just about missing your old life. It's also about the subtle ways your identity shifts and changes. You learn new customs, adopt new convictions, and gradually, you become a hybrid of your old self and your new surroundings. It's a process of growth, but it can also be a process of loss. You gain new experiences, but you also leave pieces of yourself behind. It's a strange and sometimes painful experience, this cultural displacement. It's a dynamic negotiation between belonging and longing, between holding onto the past and embracing the future. But it also reflects our ability to adapt, to rebuild, and to create a new sense of home, even when we're far from the place we started.

CHAPTER ELEVEN

SEEKING HELP

Maria told me her story, her voice soft and hesitant at first, gaining momentum as she went on. She described the stark contrast between the warmth of her community she'd left behind and the sterile, continuous whirring of machinery in the social services office. Her hands, rough from years of farm work, trembled as she showed me the worn manila folder. "My name is Maria Rodriguez," she'd said, the name sounding foreign here. In her village, she was Maria, daughter of Isabella, wife of Miguel. Here, she was just a file.

Three months she'd been in this new country, this overwhelming city. She'd arrived with such hope, her suitcase, though small, felt overflowing with dreams. Miguel was supposed to join her, as soon as she found work and a place for them. But the reality... well, it had been harsh. The language was a crippling handicap. I could see the frustration in her eyes, the way she wrestled with understanding, the way her confidence seemed to shrink with every misinterpreted word. She'd found a tiny room in a shared house, but the rent ate up almost all her savings. And jobs? They were so hard to come by, especially with her limited English. Even simple things, like buying groceries, were a huge ordeal.

Loneliness clung to her like a shadow. She missed her family, the familiar routines of her village, the smell of her mother's cooking. Here, the air was thick with exhaust fumes and an almost palpable indifference.

That day, she'd gone to the social services office, hoping for help. She'd heard it was a place where they helped newcomers. But sitting in the waiting room, surrounded by others who looked just as lost as she did, I could see the doubt creeping in. Would anyone understand? Would anyone care?

Finally, her name was called. She followed the woman into a small, sterile office. The woman spoke slowly, trying to make it easier for Maria to understand. Maria showed her documents, her passport, her work permit – those flimsy papers on which so much depended. The questions were simple, but they felt like mountains to climb.

"Where do you work?"

Maria just shook her head, her cheeks burning with shame.

"Do you have family here?"

Her eyes flickered, and I knew she was thinking of Miguel. "Not yet," she whispered.

The woman at the desk didn't give up. She explained the forms, the programs, the whole complicated process. It was daunting, a mountain of paperwork. I could see Maria's shoulders slump. Then, something wonderful happened. The woman reached across the desk and touched Maria's hand. It was just a brief touch, but it was like a spark. I saw a flicker of hope in Maria's eyes. The woman then introduced her to an interpreter, a volunteer from Maria's region. And just like that, the language barrier crumbled. Maria could finally explain everything, her fears, her hopes. She could be Maria again, not just a file.

She left the office that day, and even though she didn't have all the answers, something had changed. The tension appeared to relax somewhat. She'd taken that first step. She'd asked for help.

And in that moment of vulnerability, a tiny seed of hope had been planted in the barren landscape of her new life. It was a small thing, but it was a start. And you know, sometimes, that's all an immigrant has – a start, and the hope that somewhere, someone will understand, and someone will help.

Overcoming Stigma and Seeking Help

Coming to a new country, you carry so much – hopes, dreams, the weight of leaving everything behind. But sometimes, you also carry a burden you didn't expect: the stigma surrounding mental health. For immigrants, this stigma can be particularly heavy, making it incredibly difficult to reach out for help when we need it most. We're often told, implicitly or explicitly, to be strong, to be stoic. We're supposed to have it all together, grateful for the opportunities we've been given. Admitting we're struggling, that we're feeling distressed, anxious, or depressed, can feel like a failure, a betrayal of that image of strength. We fear being judged, not just by our own communities, but by the wider society as well. We worry that seeking help will be seen as weakness, that it will reinforce negative stereotypes about immigrants being a burden or unable to cope.

This stigma can be especially damaging because the immigrant experience itself can be incredibly stressful. We face language barriers, cultural adjustments, financial pressures, and the emotional toll of being separated from family and friends. We might experience discrimination, isolation, and estrangement. All of these factors can contribute to mental health challenges, yet the stigma prevents many of us from seeking the support we desperately need. I know, from direct experience, just how isolating that can be. For a long time, I struggled in silence. I felt ashamed, convinced that I should be able to handle everything on my own. It wasn't until I reached a breaking point that I finally realised I needed help. Taking that first step was terrifying, but it was also the bravest thing I've ever done. What I learned is that seeking help is not a sign of weakness; it's a sign of strength. It takes courage to acknowledge that you're struggling and to reach out for support. It's a sign that you're committed to your well-being, to your healing, and to building a better life for yourself.

We need to break down this stigma within our communities. We need to talk openly about mental health, to create safe spaces where people can share their experiences without fear of judgment. We need to educate ourselves about mental health resources and encourage others to seek help when they need it. We need to understand that mental health is just as important as physical health, and that seeking help is not a sign of weakness.

CHAPTER TWELVE

RESILIENCE AND HOPE

L ike two sides of a coin, resilience and hope are mutually dependent, woven into our very being. Resilience is the ability to bounce back from adversity, to withstand hardship and emerge stronger, while hope is the steadfast belief that a better future is possible, even in the face of seemingly insurmountable challenges. They feed each other, resilience providing the strength to hold onto hope, and hope fuelling the drive to persevere.

Resilience isn't about being invincible or never experiencing setbacks. It's about acknowledging the pain, the struggle, the disappointment, and choosing to move forward anyway. It's about finding inner ascendancy, and letting past experiences inform how you adapt to new realities. Resilient individuals often possess a strong sense of self-efficacy, a belief in their ability to influence their circumstances and overcome obstacles. They are problem-solvers, ingenious and versatile, able to find creative solutions to difficult situations.

Hope, on the other hand, is the light that guides us through the darkness. It's the inner voice that whispers, "Don't give up," even when everything seems hopeless. Hope isn't blind optimism or naive wishful thinking. It's a realistic assessment of the possibilities, combined with a belief in our capacity to create positive change. Hope fuels our motivation, giving us the energy to keep going when we feel like giving up. It allows us to envision a brighter future, even if it's just a glimmer on the horizon. The ability to withstand hardship and maintain optimism is vital for overcoming life's obstacles. When faced with adversity, resilience enables the strength to cope, to pivot, to survive. Hope inspires the motivation to keep moving forward, to strive for something better. Together, they create a powerful force that can help us overcome even the most daunting obstacles.

Consider the refugee fleeing war, the patient battling a serious illness, the entrepreneur facing repeated failures. In each of these situations, resilience and hope are paramount for survival and eventual triumph. Resilience allows them to endure the hardships, to cope with the trauma, to keep going even when they feel like giving up. Hope allows them to believe in a better future, to keep fighting for their dreams, to never lose sight of what they are striving for.

Cultivating resilience and hope is a lifelong process. It involves developing self-awareness, recognising our strengths, and learning from our experiences. This process includes nurturing our connections with others, building strong support networks, and finding meaning and purpose in our lives. Practicing gratitude, focusing on the positive aspects of our lives, and engaging in activities that bring us joy can also help to strengthen our resilience and cultivate hope. In a world that is often filled with uncertainty, resilience and hope are not just desirable qualities, they are requisite for our well-being and our ability to thrive. They are the inner resources that allow us to stand firm during the complexities of life, to overcome adversity, and to create a future that is filled with meaning, purpose, and joy. They are the twin engines that drive us forward on the journey of life, helping us to not just survive, but to truly live.

The Power of the Human Spirit

The power of human spirit is a phrase that is often used, but what does it really mean? It is easy to say that the human spirit is powerful, but it is another thing to actually witness it in action. I believe that the human spirit is the driving force behind all of our accomplishments, both big and small. It is what allows us to overcome obstacles, to persevere in the face of adversity, and to achieve things that we never thought possible. I have seen the power of the human spirit time and again in my life. I saw it in my sister Alero when she was battling cancer. She never gave up hope, even when things were at their worst. She fought fiercely with everything she had, and she eventually beat the disease. I saw it in my friend Gbenga who lost his job during the recession. He was devastated, but he didn't let it get him down. He picked himself up and started his own business, which is now thriving. I see it in the everyday acts of kindness and compassion that I witness all around me.

We can observe further instances of the human spirit's power in these examples:
Nelson Mandela was imprisoned for 27 years for his fight against apartheid. Yet, he never gave up hope and eventually became the first black president of South Africa.
Malala Yousafzai was shot in the head by the Taliban for speaking out for girls' education. But she survived and went on to win the Nobel Peace Prize.
Stephen Hawking was diagnosed with (Amyotrophic lateral sclerosis) ALS at the age of 21. Despite his illness, he became one of the most brilliant physicists of our time.
The survivors of the Holocaust endured unimaginable suffering, but they never gave up their humanity. They went on

to rebuild their lives and to share their stories so that the world would never forget.

The people of Ukraine demonstrating indomitable courage in the face of overwhelming force to maintain their liberty. They showed the world what it means to be courageous and resilient.

The human spirit is a powerful force that can help us achieve anything we set our minds to. It is what makes us human, and it is what makes us special. We all have the power within us to overcome any obstacle that we face. We simply need to tap into our inner strength and let our spirits soar. The power of the human spirit is a concept that refers to the extraordinary capacity of humans to overcome adversity, demonstrate capability in hellacious times, and achieve remarkable things. It encompasses qualities such as resilience, courage, perseverance, hope, and the ability to find meaning and purpose in life.

The human spirit has been celebrated in countless stories, literature, and art throughout history. It is often depicted in the accounts of individuals who have faced seemingly insurmountable challenges yet found the inner strength to rise above them. These stories inspire us and attest to our own potential to overcome obstacles and achieve our goals. The power of the human spirit is not just a theoretical concept; it is something that we can witness in the everyday lives of people around us. We see it in the determination of athletes who push themselves to their limits, the compassion of volunteers who dedicate their time to helping others, and the creativity of artists who express their emotions and ideas through their work.

The human spirit is also evident in our collective efforts to address global crises. We have seen how people from all walks of life come together to fight poverty, disease, and climate change. These efforts demonstrate the power of human cooperation and the ability to create positive change.

While the human spirit is a powerful force, it is important to remember that it is not invincible. We all experience tough times and setbacks, and it is during these times that we must draw upon our inner strength and resilience. By cultivating hope, gratitude, and a positive mindset, we can tap into the power of our human spirit and overcome any obstacle that comes our way.

Against All Odds

The immigrant experience, our experience, exemplifies the indomitable power of the human spirit and our remarkable ability to overcome adversity. It's a journey we know intimately, often undertaken with little more than hope and a burning desire to build a better life. We've lived it – leaving behind familiar landscapes, our support networks, sometimes even loved ones, embarking on a path where every step presented a new test. The language barriers, the repeated cultural adjustments, the often-difficult process of integrating into a new society – it can feel overwhelming, we know. Yet, it is in these very challenges that our strength, the strength of the human spirit, shines through.

Propelled by dreams of opportunity, freedom, or simply a safer future, we, like so many others, have displayed extraordinary resilience. We've faced obstacles head-on, transforming adversity into a catalyst for growth. We've learned new languages, acquired new skills, and navigated unfamiliar systems, all while often working tirelessly to support ourselves and our families. We understand the sheer grit and decisiveness required to rebuild a life in a new land – that tremendous endeavour, that powerful demonstration of human resilience. But it's not just about survival, is it? We, and so many like us, often thrive. We bring with us diverse perspectives, talents, and experiences that enrich our new communities. We build businesses, create jobs, and contribute to the cultural heritage of our adopted home.

From humble beginnings, we've seen many immigrants achieve remarkable success, defying expectations and proving that hard work, perseverance, and a belief in oneself can overcome even the most daunting odds.

Our story isn't just one of hardship; it's a story of triumph. It's a story of courage, resilience, and the persistent pursuit of a brighter future. It's a story that underscores the boundless capacity of the human spirit and the extraordinary ability to overcome adversity, proving that even in the face of immense challenges, hope can flourish, and dreams can be realised. It's our story, and it's a story worth telling.

CHAPTER THIRTEEN

THE MANY LAYERS OF US

A s an immigrant, I've come to understand that my identity isn't defined by just one aspect of who I am. It's a dynamic entity formed from the building blocks of my race, gender, class, religion, and nationality.

Intersectionality, a term coined by Kimberlé Crenshaw, is a framework that helps me understand how these different aspects of my identity intersect and shape my experiences in a new country. I've learned that being an immigrant isn't a singular experience. A wealthy white European immigrant will likely face different challenges than a poor Black immigrant seeking assylum from a war-torn region. Even within the same immigrant community, a woman may face discrimination that a man doesn't, due to gender roles and societal expectations.

Intersectionality has also helped me recognise the unique challenges faced by those with multiple marginalised identities. For example, an immigrant woman of colour may face both sexism and racism, making her experience significantly different from that of a white immigrant woman or an immigrant man of colour. Understanding intersectionality has been empowering. It's given me a language to articulate the inexplicabilities of my own experience and to connect with others who share similar intersections of identity. It's also helped me to be more aware of the privileges and disadvantages that come with different aspects of my identity.

In a world that often tries to simplify and categorize people, intersectionality teaches us that everyone's story is unique and multifaceted. It's a powerful tool for building empathy, understanding, and solidarity across different communities.

Intersectionality and Immigration

Immigration is a multifaceted journey, an interplay of a range of personal aspirations, economic necessities, and often, forced displacement. It's rarely a singular experience, however. Instead, it intersects with a multitude of other social justice issues, creating unique and often compounded troubles for individuals who embody these identities. Understanding these intersections is not just an academic exercise; it's a prerequisite for creating truly equitable and inclusive societies that recognise and address the diverse realities of immigrant lives.

1. Gender and Immigration
Immigration has a pronounced gender dimension, with women and men often migrating for different reasons and facing distinct challenges. Women frequently migrate for economic opportunities, to join family members, or to escape gender-based violence, including female genital mutilation, forced marriage, and honour killings. However, their experiences are often shaped by patriarchal influences both in their home countries and their adopted lands. They may face exploitation in domestic work, agriculture, or the sex industry, where they may be subjected to low wages, poor working conditions, and limited legal protection.

Furthermore, cultural and religious norms in their adopted country can further restrict their autonomy, access to education, healthcare, and other viable resources. Transgender and gender non-conforming immigrants face even greater vulnerability, often experiencing discrimination and violence due to their gender identity.

2. Sexuality and Immigration

LGBTQ+ individuals may face persecution in their home countries due to laws or social norms that criminalise or discriminate against same-sex relationships or gender non-conformity. Seeking asylum based on sexual orientation or gender identity can be an unfathomably difficult and often traumatic process, requiring individuals to prove a well-founded fear of persecution. Even when granted asylum, LGBTQ+ immigrants may face challenges in obtaining legal recognition of their same-sex marriages or partnerships in their adopted country, affecting their access to benefits and rights. Social isolation and discrimination are also common experiences, as they struggle with building community and finding support in a new cultural context. The intersection of sexuality with race and ethnicity can further compound these challenges, as LGBTQ+ immigrants of colour may experience discrimination within both LGBTQ+ and racial/ethnic communities.

3. Disability and Immigration

Immigrants with disabilities face a unique set of challenges as they navigate the immigration process and settle into their adopted country. Access to healthcare, rehabilitation services, and disability-related support can be severely limited, especially if they lack language proficiency or are unfamiliar with the healthcare system. Language and cultural barriers can further complicate the process of navigating bureaucratic procedures, applying for disability benefits, and accessing necessary resources. Discrimination and stigma related to disability can be compounded by xenophobia and anti-immigrant sentiment, making social inclusion and economic opportunity even harder to achieve. The intersection of disability with race, gender, and class can further exacerbate these challenges, as individuals may face multiple forms of marginalisation.

4. Race and Immigration
Immigrants often face racial discrimination in various aspects of life, including employment, housing, education, and dealings with law enforcement. Xenophobia and anti-immigrant sentiment can be closely intertwined with racism, targeting immigrants with prejudice, hate speech, and hate crimes. Racial bias can amplify the difficulties immigrants face due to cultural and linguistic differences, thereby creating further impediments to integration and social mobility. The intersection of race with other identities, such as gender, sexuality, and disability, can create unique forms of discrimination. For example, immigrant women of colour may face both sexism and racism in the workplace, while immigrant men of colour may be disproportionately targeted by racial profiling and police brutality.

5. The Interwoven Nature of Oppression
It's crucial to understand that these intersections are not mutually exclusive. An immigrant woman of colour with a disability, for example, embodies multiple marginalised identities and may face a unique set of challenges that are not simply the sum of each individual identity. She may experience gendered racism, ableism, and xenophobia simultaneously, facing discrimination in employment, housing, and healthcare. Her experiences are shaped by these intersecting oppressions, and any attempt to address her needs must consider this intersectionality.

Moving Forward

Addressing the intersectional challenges faced by immigrants requires a holistic and strategic approach. Policies and programs must be designed with an intersectional lens, recognising the unique needs of individuals with intersecting identities. To achieve this, culturally competent services are instrumental, ensuring that service providers are aware of the specific needs faced by immigrants from diverse backgrounds. Advocacy and representation are crucial, ensuring that immigrants with intersecting identities have a voice in the policies and programs that affect their lives. Finally, building inclusive communities where immigrants feel welcome and supported is essential for their well-being and integration. By understanding and addressing the complex and often challenging experiences that shape immigrant lives, we can create a more just and equitable society for all.

CHAPTER FOURTEEN

THE CONTRIBUTIONS OF IMMIGRANTS

T he city's symphony of sounds, the rich palette of its cultures, the tantalising flavours of its food—these are all melodies in the enduring song of immigrant contributions. Like many who came before me, I arrived with dreams, my whole life packed into a bag, and my heart filled with optimism. And like so many others, I found that this country, while sometimes challenging, offered opportunities to build a new life and contribute to something larger than myself. It's easy to talk about the big things – the groundbreaking innovations, the businesses built from the ground up, the Nobel Prize winners. And yes, immigrants have undeniably made their mark in these arenas. But for me, the true measure of our contribution lies in the everyday, the often-unseen progress that we inculcate into the entire society. It's in the small family restaurant where the aroma of spices from my homeland fills the air, introducing new flavours to curious palates. It's in the classroom where I share stories of my culture with children, fostering understanding and empathy. It's in the hospital where I work alongside colleagues from all corners of the globe, caring for patients and sharing our expertise. It's in the community garden where I cultivate vegetables from my native land, sharing the harvest with my neighbours. We bring more than just our skills and labour. We bring our perspectives, our traditions, our briskness. We bring a different way of looking at the world, a different rhythm to the city's pulse. We challenge assumptions, broaden horizons, and enrich the cultural landscape overall.

The journey of an immigrant is rarely easy. But through it all, their determination remains strong to succeed, to build a better future for ourselves and our families. And it's this very determination, this grit, that fuels our contributions. We are not just newcomers. We are builders, creators, innovators, and dreamers. We are an integral part of this society, shaping its present and contributing to its future. And while our stories are diverse and our experiences unique, we are united by the desire to contribute, to belong, and to make this place, our new home, a little bit brighter.

The Unsung Heroes of Progress

The narrative of progress is often told with grand strokes, focusing on inventors, visionaries, and leaders. But behind many of these celebrated figures, and forming the core root of advancement, are the unsung heroes of progress: immigrants. Their stories, often untold, are testaments to doggedness, ingenuity, and possibility. Let's explore the many facets of immigrant contributions.

Economy

Immigrants often revitalise communities experiencing population decline, injecting new life and bolstering local economies through their spending and entrepreneurial spirit. Their contributions extend beyond launching new businesses; they also reinvigorate existing ones. Immigrants bring fresh perspectives, global market knowledge, and a strong work ethic, frequently leading to increased productivity and innovation within established companies. London's renowned curry houses, many immigrant-run, exemplify this, contributing significantly to both the city's vibrant culinary scene and its economy. Moreover, immigrants are essential to key sectors. The tech industry, for example, thrives on the influx of skilled programmers and engineers from around the globe, driving advancements in software development and artificial intelligence. Immigrants also fill critical labour shortages in sectors like healthcare and agriculture. Within the NHS, for instance, a substantial proportion of doctors and nurses are foreign-born, playing a vital role in ensuring the smooth operation of this indispensable institution.

From the 19th-century Highland Railway in Scotland through to today's HS2 high-speed lines, immigrants have played a pivotal role in building and maintaining the UK's vital rail and bridge infrastructure. The construction of the Highland Railway, a crucial 19th-century transport link, relied heavily on the prowess and sheer hard work of Irish navvies. Facing harsh conditions and dangerous work, they laid tracks, dug tunnels, and constructed bridges across challenging terrains, including the Scottish Highlands and demanding projects in northern England. Decades later, in the 1950s and 1960s, British Railways actively recruited workers from Eastern Europe and the West Indies to address labour shortages and assist in the rebuilding and modernisation of the network. Their efforts were vital in the post-war era. This legacy of immigrant involvement continues to the present day.

Immigrants have been instrumental in the construction and maintenance of many of the UK's iconic bridges, from Victorian-era structures to modern marvels. Their expertise in structural engineering, welding, and other specialised trades is crucial for ensuring the continued safety and functionality of these remarkable links. Currently, immigrant engineers and construction workers are contributing their skills to major infrastructure projects like HS2, playing a key role in the design and construction of new high-speed rail lines and bridges. These contributions are not merely a historical footnote. Immigrants continue to be essential to maintaining and improving this critical infrastructure, ensuring the safe and efficient movement of people and goods across the country. Their ongoing involvement underscores the enduring and vital nature of their contributions to the UK's transport network.

Healthcare
The National Health Service (NHS) relies heavily on immigrant workers, who constitute a substantial proportion of its doctors, nurses, and other healthcare professionals. These individuals provide essential care and services to patients across the United Kingdom, and their multilingual skills and cultural sensitivity are invaluable assets, ensuring effective communication and culturally competent care for diverse patient populations.

Furthermore, immigrant doctors and nurses are often more willing to serve in underserved rural areas, guaranteeing access to healthcare for communities that might otherwise struggle to find qualified professionals.

Beyond direct patient care, immigrant scientists and researchers make significant contributions to medical breakthroughs and advancements in healthcare, leading to improved treatments and better patient outcomes for everyone.

Culture
From the tantalising aromas of Indian curries to the comforting warmth of Italian pasta, the diverse food selections brought by immigrants have become an integral and celebrated part of British culture. The UK's dynamic food scene illustrates the transformative impact of immigration, with newcomers not only introducing entirely new dishes but also subtly influencing and transforming existing British cuisine. This culinary fusion has resulted in exciting and innovative flavours now enjoyed by

everyone, a delicious symbol of cultural exchange. Beyond the realm of food, immigrant artists, musicians, writers, and filmmakers contribute diverse narratives and perspectives to the UK's cultural landscape. Their work enriches the arts scene, fostering cross-cultural understanding and broadening horizons for all. These contributions are further amplified by the vibrant festivals and traditions that immigrants have introduced, adding exciting new dimensions to the UK's cultural calendar. These celebrations create invaluable opportunities for communities to come together, share experiences, and celebrate the richness of diversity.

Among the most iconic examples is the Notting Hill Carnival, a vibrant explosion of Caribbean culture, particularly British-Caribbean heritage. With its dazzling costumes, pulsating music, and irresistible aromas of Caribbean cuisine, the Carnival stands as a testament to the community's fortitude and spirit.

Chinese New Year, celebrated in cities across the UK with large Chinese communities, brings colourful parades, lion and dragon dances, and delicious traditional food, marking a time for family, reflection, and welcoming good fortune.

Vaisakhi, the Sikh harvest festival, is marked by vibrant processions, energetic Bhangra dancing, and the sharing of food in Gurdwara langars, a celebration of community, faith, and the harvest.

While not strictly an "immigrant" festival in the strictest sense, the large Irish diaspora in the UK has made St. Patrick's Day a major celebration across the country, complete with parades, music, and of course, Guinness.

Diwali, the Hindu, Sikh, and Jain Festival of Lights, illuminates homes with lamps and fireworks, symbolising the triumph of good over evil and marking a time for family and new beginnings.

Eid al-Fitr and Eid al-Adha, important religious holidays for Muslims, are celebrated with special prayers, family gatherings, and the sharing of food.

Hanukkah, the Jewish Festival of Lights, is observed by lighting a menorah each night for eight nights, commemorating the rededication of the Second Temple of Jerusalem. These festivals, alongside numerous others, seamlessly integrate to form the vibrant and varied cultural landscape of modern Britain.

Science and Technology

Immigrant scientists significantly enrich the UK's scientific landscape in numerous ways. Their continued connections with their countries of origin often facilitate international research collaborations, benefiting not only the UK's scientific community but also contributing to global scientific progress. They play a vital role in STEM education, inspiring and mentoring the next generation of scientists and engineers. Their diverse backgrounds and experiences create a richer learning environment, promoting innovation and fostering a more dynamic and creative academic atmosphere. Furthermore, immigrant scientists and researchers are often at the forefront of addressing critical global crises, including climate change, disease outbreaks, and food security, lending their expertise to finding solutions that benefit all of humanity.

Immigrants and the Shaping of America

While immigrant-founded giants like Google capture headlines, the true story of immigrant entrepreneurship lies in the everyday businesses they build. Immigrants are the driving force behind dry cleaners, restaurants, construction firms, and a vast array of small enterprises that form the backbone of local economies. Often taking risks where others hesitate, they revitalise neighbourhoods and generate jobs in communities that need them most. Beyond entrepreneurship, immigrants are significantly overrepresented in STEM fields, and their contributions extend far beyond Silicon Valley. They are the engineers designing our bridges, the scientists developing life-saving medicines, and the researchers pushing the boundaries of technology in universities and laboratories nationwide. This infusion of talent fuels American innovation and maintains the nation's competitive edge on the global stage. Furthermore, as the US population ages, immigrants play a vital role in addressing critical labour shortages, particularly in sectors like healthcare and elder care. They provide key services that ensure the well-being of older Americans, contributing to a more secure and supported aging population.

The diverse flavours of American cuisine exemplify the power of blending. Consider the origins of dishes we consider quintessentially American: pizza, hot dogs, even apple pie—all have immigrant roots. American food is a delicious, ever-evolving blend of influences, constantly being reshaped and revitalised by new arrivals. Immigrants don't simply open restaurants; they introduce novel ingredients, cooking techniques, and flavours that gradually become an indispensable part of the national palate. This innovative spirit extends far beyond the kitchen.

Immigrant artists push the boundaries of American art in all its forms. They introduce and popularise new musical styles, like salsa and hip-hop, that often become mainstream. In literature and film, they challenge traditional portrayals, offering fresh and often vital frames of reference for the American experience. From vibrant murals that enliven urban landscapes to intricate crafts that preserve cultural heritage, they introduce new forms of visual art, enriching the cultural landscape for everyone.

The impact of immigration is also evident in the evolution of American English. Immigrants contribute to its dynamic nature, introducing new words and expressions that often become part of the common lexicon. Furthermore, they bring diverse philosophical and intellectual traditions, sparking important new debates and enriching the national discourse with a wider range of ideas.

Immigrants frequently establish robust community organisations grounded in shared language, culture, or faith. These vital hubs provide crucial support for newcomers, facilitating integration into American society while simultaneously preserving cherished cultural heritage. They become centres of social connection and civic engagement, strengthening the fabric of their communities. Furthermore, immigrants often maintain strong ties to their countries of origin, fostering trade, cultural exchange, and even contributing to diplomatic relations. In this way, they act as bridges between the United States and the world, promoting understanding and cooperation. The challenges inherent in building a new life in a foreign land demand immense vigour and perseverance, qualities that ultimately enhance the American spirit of innovation and hard work.

Beyond the Famous Names

It's important to remember that the vast majority of immigrant contributions aren't made by famous figures. They're the everyday acts of millions of people: the doctor who cares for your child, the entrepreneur who opens a local business, the engineer who designs a safer bridge. It's in these everyday contributions that the true impact of immigration is felt. By understanding the full scope of immigrant contributions, we can recognise the vital role they play in shaping the dynamism and prosperity of nations around the world.

CHAPTER FIFTEEN

VOICES THROUGH THE JOURNEY

The silence in my small London flat is a heavy blanket, one I pull tighter around myself each night. It's a far cry from the boisterous laughter of my boys, the gentle hum of my wife's presence as she moved through our home. Here, the only sounds are the distant wail of a siren, the rhythmic tick of the clock on the mantelpiece – each a stark reminder of the time passing, the miles stretching, the life I've temporarily left behind.

The decision to come here was not taken lightly. It was a sacrifice, a calculated risk for a better future for my family. Years. The word echoes in my mind like a hollow drumbeat. Years separated from the very people who give my life meaning. What once felt like a fresh start is now a distant echo, drowned out by a gnawing loneliness that settles deep in my bones. Video calls offer glimpses, fragmented moments of their lives continuing without me, and while I cherish them, they also amplify the ache of absence. I see my sons growing, their voices deepening, my wife's smile holding a hint of weariness I can't soothe with a hug.

In this landscape of solitude, Joie became a beacon. We met at a community event, both of us feeling like outsiders in different ways. She was warm, with a ready laugh and an understanding gaze that seemed to see past the surface of my carefully constructed composure. We started talking, tentatively at first, sharing stories of our families, our struggles, our hopes. Soon, those conversations became longer, more frequent. We found solace in each other's company, a shared space where the weight of our individual burdens felt a little lighter.

With Joie, I could speak freely about the things I kept bottled up – the constant worry about my family, the pressure to succeed, the stress of change. She listened without judgment, offering empathy and practical advice. We explored the city together, discovering hidden corners and shared moments of joy amidst the everyday. A cup of coffee in a bustling café, a walk along the Thames on a crisp autumn evening, a shared laugh at a silly joke – these small moments became anchors in my lonely existence. She became a special friend, a confidante, someone who understood the uniqueness of my situation without needing lengthy explanations.

But loneliness, I've come to realize, is a dangerous beast. It gnaws at your defences, leaving you vulnerable to the unexpected currents of emotion. Slowly, subtly, something shifted. The comfort I found in Joie's presence began to morph into something else. A warmth that extended beyond friendship, a longing for her company that felt different from the simple desire for connection. I started noticing the way her eyes crinkled when she smiled, the gentle touch of her hand on my arm, and these small gestures sparked feelings within me that I knew were wrong, inappropriate, a betrayal of the life I had built and the love I held for my wife.

The realization hit me with the force of a cold shower. These burgeoning emotions were a product of my vulnerability, a desperate grasping for connection in the face of overwhelming loneliness. They weren't a true reflection of my heart's deepest desires. I wouldn't trade the years of love and commitment with my wife, the joy of watching my sons grow, for these fleeting, unsolicited feelings. The thought of jeopardizing the precious friendship I had found with Joie for something that felt like a mirage was unbearable.

The internal conflict became a heavy weight in my chest, a constant hum of anxiety. I knew I had to address it, not only for my own peace of mind but also out of respect for Joie. The thought of hurting her, of leading her on, was deeply unsettling. So, I asked her to meet, my heart pounding with a mixture of fear and resolve.

Over a quiet lunch, the words felt clumsy and inadequate as I tried to explain the dances of my emotions. I spoke of the profound loneliness that had become my constant companion, the vulnerability it had created within me. I explained how much I valued her friendship, how her presence had been a lifeline in a difficult time. And then, I confessed the unwanted feelings that had begun to surface, emphasizing that they were a consequence of my emotional state, not a reflection of any intention to betray our friendship or my commitment to my family.

It was a difficult conversation, filled with hesitant words and long pauses. I saw a flicker of hurt in her eyes, and the guilt washed over me. I tried to make her understand that these feelings were a burden to me, something I was actively fighting against. I reiterated that my intention was never to hurt her, that the depth of my loneliness had created a fertile ground for these emotions to take root.

The aftermath of that conversation hung in the air, thick with unspoken words and uncertain futures. I don't know what the future holds for our friendship. I hope that Joie can understand my vulnerability, my desperate need for connection that had inadvertently led to this complicated situation. I pray that our bond, built on genuine care and shared experiences, can withstand this uncomfortable truth.

The loneliness in my flat persists, but now it's tinged with a different kind of ache – the fear of losing a dear friend, the regret of allowing my emotions to stray into forbidden territory.

The journey of an immigrant is fraught with challenges, many of them unseen. Loneliness is one such invisible burden, a silent predator that can prey on the most vulnerable parts of ourselves. This experience has been a sobering thought of the importance of boundaries, the fragility of emotions, and the enduring strength of the love that ties me to my family across the miles. It's a lesson etched in the quiet solitude of this London flat, a lesson I will carry with me as I continue to navigate this complex and often isolating immigrant experience.

The Gift of Global Friendship

My journey began with a mix of anticipation and apprehension, a feeling familiar to many who leave their homeland, but I've been incredibly fortunate. The world I stepped into was vast and varied, where I encountered the lives of extraordinary individuals, people who have truly enriched my experience beyond measure. From every corner of the world, paths have crossed, and hearts have connected.

I remember Precious, from Nigeria. Her infectious positivity brightened even the darkest days, and she was always the first to offer a hand. Alfe Suny Ratul, with his gentle spirit told me stories of Bangladesh. Filipe, with the vibrant energy of Brazil, taught me the joy of spontaneous celebration. Joisse, from the Philippines, shared her genuine kindness, a light and strength in unfamiliar surroundings. Chico, from Bermuda, brought laughter with his easy-going charm. Michael, from Ireland, there's a warmth about him, a kindness that's immediately apparent. It's the sort of quiet, steady goodness that made me feel comfortable and valued.

Laura, with her Australian pragmatism, offered steady encouragement. Darsh, from India, shared meaningful insights and a deep sense of community. Alexander, with his courteousness and Swedish directness, showed me the value of clear communication. Helder, from Mozambique, brought a warmth that transcended language barriers. Gaz, from Syria, despite his own hardships, shared his undaunted spirit and unwavering hope. B Wani, from Angola, showed me the power of quiet determination. DJ Luca, from Italy, filled my days with music, making them carefree and joyful. Victoria, with her American ambition and openness, inspired me to pursue my dreams. Nabil, from South Africa, shared stories of doggedness and independence.

Patryk, with his Polish humour, kept me laughing. Ross, with his quintessentially English wit, made me feel at home. Kouros, from Iran, shared his passion for art and culture. Aline, with her French elegance, showed me the beauty of refined conversation. Kabita, from Nepal, shared her serene wisdom and a deep connection to nature. Benjamin, from the Republic of Congo, showed me the importance of community and shared joy. Dennis, from Albania, shared his strong sense of loyalty.

Nicholas, from St. Lucia, brought a laid-back and welcoming energy. Marcio Gomes, from Portugal, shared his passion for his cultural heritage. Fredrick, from Liberia, showed me the power of perseverance. Elliot, from New Zealand, shared his love of the outdoors and of adventure. Khalid, from Egypt, shared his knowledge and history. Panos, from Greece, shared his love of his culture and food. Yahya, from Morocco, shared his wisdom and kindness. Alex Fierro, from Canada, shared a unique and open-minded perspective. Veronica, from Spain, shared her passion for life. Earl, from Granada, shared his friendly and calming presence. Irina, from Russia, shared her patriotism and certitude. Stephen, from the Dominican Republic, didn't just show me kindness; his actions sparked a wave of generosity that inspired others to follow suit.

And then there were Noah, Emeka, Dominic, Lucas, Iris, Pedro Mendoza, Richard, Aditi, Zara, Rajin, Himanshu, and a host of others. Irrespective of where they come from, what they believe, or how they look, these individuals, in their own unique ways, loved me naturally, encouraged my dreams, respected my journey, motivated me to grow, and filled my days with joy and laughter. They helped me in ways too numerous to list.

I can truly say that I have been loved by the best.

The Strength in Our Shared Humanity

Our immigrant journey, as many of us know, involves huge changes. We leave familiar places, languages, and ways of life to figure out a new home. What's often overlooked is the bond we forge in each other, across different nationalities, religions, races, and cultures. This unity, built on shared experiences and respect, is a major positive force, helping us not just survive, but thrive. The act of migrating itself creates common ground for us. We all face similar challenges: visa processes, learning new languages, navigating unfamiliar systems, and adapting to different customs. This shared vulnerability leads to empathy and support. When we find ourselves in the same situation, regardless of where we come from, we naturally help each other out.

This connection goes beyond differences in nationality, race, or background. It's about the basic human need for connection in a foreign place. The diverse religions and cultures we bring enrich our new communities and our own lives. Imagine a community where Christians, Muslims, Hindus, Buddhists, and those with no religion live together. Instead of division, this diversity becomes a strength. We share religious festivals, learn from each other, and try new foods. This exchange broadens our perspectives and fosters respect for different viewpoints. We move beyond just tolerating differences to truly appreciating them.

This unity helps us combat the isolation that can come with being an immigrant. Leaving family and social circles is hard. But in diverse communities, we build new support systems. We find comfort in connecting with others who understand what it's like to be "different." Even with different languages, we find ways to communicate and connect through our shared experience of adapting. Moreover, this unity encourages personal growth. We're constantly exposed to different ways of thinking and living. This broadens our horizons and prompts us to question our preconceptions. Interacting with people from diverse backgrounds breaks down stereotypes and helps us understand the many different facets of people.

This constant learning builds flexibility, giving us the skills to navigate an interconnected world. The unity we find in our diversity is a key part of our positive experience. It provides a foundation of understanding, builds strong communities, fights isolation, and encourages growth.

It reminds us that despite our different backgrounds, we're united by our shared humanity and our desire for a better life. By embracing this unity, we find strength and build a richer world.

CHAPTER SIXTEEN

POLICY RECOMMENDATIONS

W hat makes policy recommendations engaging is their potential to shape our future. They're not just abstract ideas; they can lead to real-world changes that affect our lives. Whether it's a new law, a shift in funding, or a change in how services are delivered, policy recommendations can have a tangible impact. Effective recommendations are clear, specific, and persuasive. They paint a picture of the problem, propose concrete solutions, and explain why those solutions are the best way forward. They anticipate foreseeable obstacles and offer strategies to overcome them. Policy recommendations also need to resonate with people. They need to tell a story that captures the imagination and inspires action. That's why the most compelling recommendations often appeal to our values, our commitment to justice, and our hopes for a better future.

Why We Need Policies that Champion Immigrant Integration and Well-being

We need policies that champion immigrant integration and well-being not just because it's the morally right thing to do, but because it's the smart thing to do. A society that embraces and supports its immigrant population reaps significant social, economic, and cultural benefits. Conversely, neglecting the needs of immigrants creates ripple effects that negatively impact everyone.

Firstly, immigrant integration is about more than just allowing people to live within a country's borders. It is about creating pathways for them to become fully participating members of society. This includes access to language training, education, job opportunities, and affordable housing. When immigrants are given the tools to succeed, they contribute to the economy, start businesses, and fill critical labour shortages. Investing in their potential is an investment in the overall prosperity of the nation. Conversely, when immigrants are marginalised and face systemic blockages, their potential is stifled, leading to lost economic opportunities and increased social costs.

Secondly, prioritising the well-being of immigrants is crucial for building strong and cohesive communities. Immigrants often face unique challenges, including cultural adjustment, discrimination, and the trauma of displacement. Policies that address these challenges, such as access to mental health services, legal aid, and culturally sensitive support systems, are essential. When immigrants feel supported and safe, they are more likely to integrate successfully, build strong social connections, and contribute positively to their communities. Ignoring their well-being can lead to social isolation, mental health issues, and even radicalisation, all of which undermine social cohesion.

Thirdly, championing immigrant integration and well-being reflects our shared values of fairness, equality, and opportunity. It's about recognising the inherent dignity of all individuals, regardless of their origin or background. Policies that promote inclusion and combat discrimination create a more just and equitable society for everyone. When we welcome and support immigrants, we send a powerful message about who we are as a nation and what we stand for.

Finally, the demographics of many countries are changing. Immigration is a reality, and it's not going away. Rather than viewing immigration as a threat, we should recognise it as an opportunity. By implementing forward-thinking policies that prioritise integration and well-being, we can harness the talents and contributions of immigrants to build a stronger, more vibrant, and more prosperous future for all. Investing in immigrants is not just an act of compassion; it's an investment in our collective future.

CHAPTER SEVENTEEN

A CALL TO ACTION

The worn soles of my shoes whisper stories of journeys, of borders crossed and oceans traversed, of a life left behind and a new one tentatively embraced. I stand here, not just as an individual, but as a testament to the spirit of tenacity that seeks refuge, opportunity, and a place to belong. And I implore you, listen. Listen not with the ears of judgement, but with the heart of compassion. The narrative surrounding immigration is often painted with broad strokes of fear and misunderstanding. We are reduced to statistics, to faceless masses, to political pawns. But beneath the labels and the rhetoric, we are human beings, just like you.

We are mothers and fathers, children and grandparents, teachers and artists, builders and dreamers. We carry within us the legacy of our past, the hopes of our future, and the resolute belief in the possibility of a better life.

Empathy, that often-elusive virtue, is the cornerstone of understanding. It is the ability to walk in another's shoes, to feel their pain, to share their joy. Imagine leaving everything you know- your home, your culture, your language- to embark on a perilous journey into the unknown. Imagine facing prejudice, discrimination, and the constant fear of deportation. Imagine striving to build a life in a society that often views you with suspicion and hostility.

Understanding transcends mere empathy. It requires a willingness to learn, scrutinise our preconceived notions, and acknowledge the multifaceted realities of immigration. It means recognising the entrenched injustices that force people to flee their homelands- poverty, violence, persecution, environmental factors. This understanding also encompasses the contributions that immigrants make to our societies- enriching our cultures, strengthening our economies, and filling vital labour shortages. It means understanding the inherent dignity and worth of every person, regardless of their origin or status.

Solidarity is the active expression of empathy and understanding. It is the willingness to stand alongside immigrant communities, to amplify their voices, and to advocate for their rights. It is the courage to confront xenophobia and racism, to speak out against injustice, and to create a more inclusive and welcoming society. It is about building bridges, not walls. It is about acknowledging that our shared humanity transcends any differences that may divide us.

Let us move beyond the divisive rhetoric and embrace a narrative of hope and possibility. Let us recognise the robustness and resolve of immigrant communities, their determination to build a better future for themselves and their children. Let us celebrate the diversity that enriches our societies and makes us stronger. Let us remember that the story of immigration is not just a story of hardship and tribulation, but also a story of courage, fortitude, and the spirit within us all that bears all things. Let us, together, build a world where every person, regardless of their origin, can thrive and reach their full potential. Let us answer this call to action and build a more just and compassionate world for all.

CHAPTER EIGHTEEN

THE LANGUAGE OF THE HEART

Words may falter, tongues may stray,
But deeper language finds its way.
The language of the heart's desire,
The warmth of love, the burning fire.
A smile, a touch, a helping hand,
A bridge across the shifting sand.
Shared laughter, tears that freely flow,
Emotions that transcend and grow.
Though accents change, and phrases bend,
The human spirit knows no end.
In every glance, a story lies,
Reflected in each other's eyes.
For in the silence, hearts can meet,
And find a rhythm, bittersweet.
The language of the soul takes flight,
And fills the world with love and light.

CHAPTER NINETEEN

LETTERS TO MY FAMILY

My Dearest Sunshine,

With every beat of my heart across these separating miles, words seem inadequate to truly express the magnitude of how intensely I miss you. My soul reached out and saw you, recognised the light that you are, even before fate physically brought us together. There is absolutely no doubt in my mind, deep within my spirit, that you are a precious, irreplaceable gift, bestowed upon me by the grace of Almighty God Himself. This sacred gift, I promise you, I will cherish, guard, and hold dear for every single one of my remaining days.

Do you remember the moment I finally settled into that seat on the plane bound for the United Kingdom? The crushing weight of the decision, the reality of the distance that was about to open between us, hit me with staggering force. In the quiet solitude at the outset of my time here, far from your comforting presence and the familiar warmth of home, I often found myself weeping, the tears a quiet manifestation of the ache in my soul. I knew, intellectually, that this journey would be one filled with new experiences, challenges, and perhaps, even moments of deep uncertainty. Yet, even then, a steadfast conviction resided within me, a whisper from the depths of my heart, that God was walking this path with me, and that ultimately, victory and purpose would emerge from the struggle.

And oh, how exceedingly thankful I am to God. He has been our constant anchor, the steadfast presence that never for a moment abandoned us as a family, especially navigating the tumultuous waves of chaos that, by His miraculous intervention, have now become part of our testimony, a victorious story we can share. He was there, always there, even when we felt most alone, guiding us through the darkest valleys. I must tell you, my love, it was a particularly difficult and agonizing period for me when you fell ill back home, coinciding almost exactly with my own struggle to find work here – a period of unemployment that stretched on for what felt like an eternity. The helplessness I felt, being so far away, unable to simply be there to care for you, was a unique torment. The thought, the terrifying possibility, that anything could happen to you, or any of our precious children, while I was absent – I honestly would not know how to bear that grief, how to navigate life without the intolerable weight of self-blame for the distance. There were other times too, many times, when isolation closed in on me, leaving me feeling like a man utterly alone in this foreign land, as if I had no home, no family, no one who truly belonged to me here in the United Kingdom.

My queen, every soul undoubtedly has a collection of stories to tell, composed of the moments and experiences that make up their life. But as I reflect deeply on my own journey, a powerful conviction has settled within me: that it is undeniably true that "people make people to tell stories." Understanding this, internalizing this truth, has brought me to a firm resolution within my own heart. I, Lawrence Thompson, am resolved to live my life in such a way that my actions, my resilience, and my faith will give people genuine, uplifting testimonies and goodness to share, rather than create stories of hardship for them.

My dearest Sunshine, it is also important for you to understand a harsh reality faced by many men who cross the shores from Africa to Europe. It is a path fraught with immense pressure, complex temptations, and often, a difficult choice. In essence, a man often finds himself compelled to become one of two things: a "beast" or a "lamb." The man who tragically becomes a "beast" often succumbs to the corrosive forces around him, allowing greed, jealousy, and difficult circumstances to strip away his integrity. Sadly, this is sometimes fuelled by the very people who should offer support, with relatives back home or even here seeking to take advantage of his new situation. Alternatively, and perhaps equally tragically, some men, having made the challenging journey across, choose to abandon their responsibilities and the sincere love of their families back home, opting instead to start entirely new lives here, building new relationships and even new families, as if the past simply ceases to exist. It is a stark and often painful reality in the lives of many migrants.

But as for me, my love, I hold the firm conviction of the sacred and irreplaceable importance of a husband in the life of his wife, and the absolutely foundational role of a father in the lives of his children. These are not roles I take lightly, nor ones I would ever trade for fleeting opportunities or personal convenience. I have consciously chosen, and will continue to choose every single day, not to abandon my family for any poor trade-offs this life abroad might offer, nor to betray the deep, sincere, and steadfast love you, my Sunshine, have so generously shown me.

My greatest aspiration, my unceasing prayer, is simply that I may live and conduct myself in such a manner that I am truly the kind of man you are genuinely proud to have as your husband.

You are, and will forever be, the guiding light etched deeply within my heart.

With all my love and devotion,
Your hubby,
Lawrence Thompson

◆◆◆

Dear Jayden,
How are you doing? I miss you so much. You're such a wonderful boy. I know you miss me too, and I'm doing everything I can to bring us all together again. I'm confident that God has already made it happen, and we'll be reunited soon.

Jayden, it's been three years since I left, and I know deep down you must wonder why daddy hasn't come home. I understand how difficult this has been for you. One day, I hope you will understand that this decision, though not easy, was made because I believe it was the best thing for your future, your mother's well-being, and the happiness of our family, including Gerald. Please know that I love you dearly. I also want you to know that your mom loves you very much, and she's doing her best to care for you and Gerald. Always respect and listen to her. Make sure you look out for Gerald. He's your younger brother, and you're his protector. Always show respect to Grandpa, Grandma, your uncles, and aunts.

I know you're a good, smart, and intelligent boy. Pay attention in school and take your studies seriously. I'm certain we'll be together again very soon. When we are, I'll tell you stories about my experiences here and how God helped me overcome challenges. Thinking of you, Gerald, and your mom gave me strength to keep going, no matter what I faced. I'm grateful for the struggles I've endured because you, my son Jayden, will learn valuable lessons from them.

Jayden, you're the best son a father could ask for, and I'll always love you. I hope to be the kind of man you'll be proud to call Dad.

See you soon!
Love always, Dad

◆ ◆ ◆

Dearest Gerald,
I'm so happy to be writing to you! I know you're reading well by now.

Gerald, I want you to focus on your schoolwork, both in class and at home. Don't worry, I'll get you and Jayden new phones soon. Know that Mommy, Grandma, and Grandpa love you very much. That's why I want you to keep being the good boy you are.

You and Jayden are both strong and smart, and I see so much potential in both of you. You're the best! I pray for you often, and I'm confident we'll be reunited soon. I'll share stories of my journey with you, and I hope you'll learn from them.

I want you and Jayden to be the best of brothers and friends. No more fighting, okay? I miss you all terribly, but we'll be together again soon.

I love you, Gerald, always and forever. I hope to be the kind of father of whom you'll be proud.

See you soon,
Love, Dad.

CHAPTER TWENTY

LETTERS FROM HOME

My Dearest Hero,
How are you doing? It feels like a lifetime since we last held each other, even though I know it hasn't been that long in the grand scheme of things. Still, three years is a long stretch, especially when you're missing the other half of your heart.

Remember all those hopeful talks we had before you left? The dreams of a better life in the UK, the plans for Jayden, Gerald, and me to join you and build a new future together? Those dreams keep me going, they truly do.

I miss you terribly, my love. There isn't a day that goes by when I don't think of you, wish you were here to share a meal, to help with the boys' homework, or simply to hold me in your arms at the end of a long day. Your calls and the money you send are a lifeline, a constant reminder that you haven't forgotten us, and for that, I am eternally grateful. It allows us to keep going, to pay the bills and put food on the table.

But life here without you is… hard. It's more than just missing your presence; it's the constant weight of responsibility that rests solely on my shoulders. Every decision, big or small, I have to make on my own. From Jayden's school issues to Gerald's sudden fever last month, there's no one here to share the worry, to offer a different perspective, or simply to lend a hand.

Sometimes, I feel like I'm juggling a dozen balls at once, and I'm constantly afraid of dropping one. Being both mother and father to our boys is exhausting, both physically and emotionally. They miss you too, you know. Jayden sometimes gets quiet and withdrawn, and Gerald often asks when daddy will be back to play football with him. It breaks my heart that I can't give them that.

There are days when I feel so incredibly lonely. The evenings are the worst. After the boys are asleep and the house is quiet, the silence screams your absence. There's no one to share my thoughts with, no one to laugh with about the day's little absurdities, no one to simply sit beside in comfortable silence. I miss our conversations, your advice, your comforting presence.

I know you're working incredibly hard over there, trying to build a foundation for us. I understand the sacrifices you're making, and I admire your strength and determination. Please know that I am so proud of you. But sometimes, the waiting feels endless, and the challenges feel overwhelming.

But I needed to share the weight I carry. It's the burden of your physical absence, the day-to-day reality of managing everything alone while yearning for my husband. Some days are harder than others, and lately, the missing you part feels especially heavy.

We are counting the moments until we can finally close this distance. Jayden and Gerald send you the biggest hugs and loudest kisses they can muster. They talk about you all the time.

Know that I love you more than words can say and I am so proud of you. Keep dreaming for us, my love, and know that we are dreaming right alongside you.

All my love, always,
Sunshine

◆◆◆

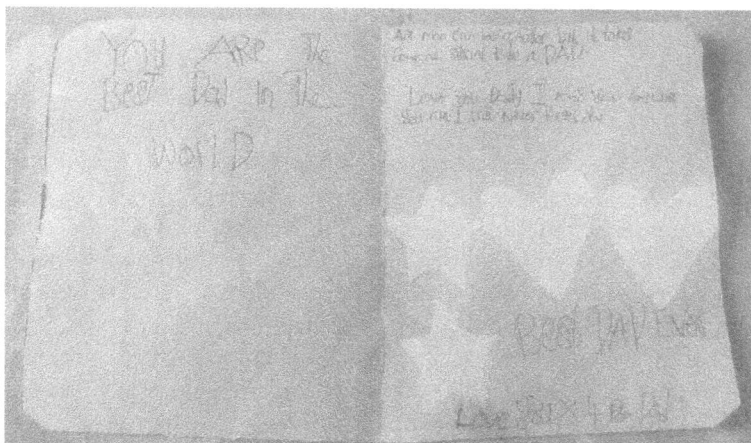

"You are the best dad in the world. Any man can be a father, but it takes someone special to be a dad. Love you daddy I miss you. Anywhere you are I will never forget you. **Best dad ever. Love you x 4 dad.**"

CHAPTER TWENTY-ONE

RESOURCES AND SUPPORT

A rriving in a new country is... overwhelming. Exciting, yes, but mostly overwhelming. But "here" is a whole new world. And finding your footing? That is the real challenge. One of the first lessons I learned, and I learned it quickly, is that you cannot do this alone. You absolutely need resources and support. It's not a sign of weakness; it's a sign of wisdom. Think of it like this: you are climbing a mountain, and you need ropes, guides, and fellow climbers to reach the summit. Resources and support are my ropes and my guides in this new land. But where do you even start? It feels like being thrown into the deep end of a pool when you barely know how to float. My first instinct was to grasp for anything that looked solid. And thankfully, there were lifelines, if you knew where to look.

The Official Channels

My visa information packet, thankfully, was not just filled with legalese. It pointed me towards government websites and organisations designed specifically to help newcomers like me. This was like striking gold. These official channels were the

bedrock of my support system. They supplied crucial services, often free or subsidised, that were lifesavers in those early days:
Information and Orientation: Websites and workshops explained everything from opening a bank account to understanding my rights as a resident. They demystified the bureaucracy and gave me a roadmap for settling in.

Language Classes: Even if I had some basic language skills, official language classes were invaluable. They weren't just about grammar; they were about understanding idioms, social etiquettes, and building confidence to communicate in everyday situations. And what's more, they connected me with other newcomers also learning the ropes.

Job Search Assistance: Finding work is paramount. Government-funded employment services helped me translate my qualifications to the local market, write a resume in the correct format, and practice for interviews. They even conducted workshops on understanding workplace culture, which is often very different from what I was used to.

Housing Support: Finding affordable housing in a new city can be brutal. These services provided information on tenant rights, helped me understand the rental market, and sometimes even connected me with temporary or transitional housing options.

Healthcare Information: Navigating a new healthcare system is incredibly stressful. These resources explained how to get health insurance, find a family doctor, and understand emergency services. Knowing where to go and what to do in a health crisis brought immense peace of mind.

Community Organisations

Beyond the official channels, I discovered the incredible power of community organisations. These are often grassroots groups, run by people who have been in my shoes. They form the backbone of support for immigrants:

Cultural Centres: Organisations representing my own cultural or ethnic background were a haven. They delivered a taste of home, a space to connect with people who understood my culture, and often provided services tailored to my community, like translation or help understanding specific cultural norms in this new country.

Settlement Agencies (Non-Profit): These are often smaller, more localized versions of the government services. They offer personalised support, mentorship programs, and a more intimate setting to ask questions and build connections. They felt less like an official institution and more like a friendly neighbour offering a hand.

Religious Institutions: For many, religious communities instil a crucial sense of acceptance and support. Churches, mosques, temples – they often host social events, language classes, and informal networks for support within their faith community.

The Power of Connection

The most powerful support often comes from informal networks:

Online Communities: Facebook groups, online forums, and social media groups for immigrants in my city were a goldmine of information and connection. People shared tips, advice, and even just gave words of encouragement. It was comforting to know I wasn't alone in navigating these complexities.

Fellow Immigrants: Talking to people who were a little further along in their journey was incredibly helpful. They could share practical advice based on their own experiences, offer encouragement, and just understand what I was going through in a way that others couldn't. These connections became some of my closest friendships.

Local Friends and Neighbours: Opening myself up to connecting with locals, even if it felt daunting at first, was a game-changer. Building relationships with people who were born and raised here gave me insights into the culture, helped me practice the language, and broadened my support network beyond just fellow immigrants.

Proactive Searching and Asking for Help

Discovering these resources wasn't always easy. It took proactive searching, a willingness to ask for help, and a bit of persistence.

Online Searches: Google was my best friend! Searching for "immigrant resources", "settlement services", "cultural organisations" led me to countless websites and organisations.

Asking Questions: At every point of contact – at the airport, at the immigration office, even just chatting with people I met – I wasn't afraid to ask "Where can I find help with…?". People are often willing to point you in the right direction if you just ask.

Visiting Community Centres and Libraries: These places often have information brochures, bulletin boards, and staff who can direct you to relevant resources. Libraries, in particular, are often hubs of information and community support.

It is Not a Straight Path, But You're Not Alone

Finding my feet in this new land is still a journey. There are days that are tough, days I feel lost and buried. But knowing that there are resources and support systems available, knowing I'm not alone in this, makes all the difference. It's like having a safety net, knowing that if I stumble, there are hands ready to help me up. These resources proved more than practical assistance; they are about building a sense of belonging, fostering hope, and empowering me to build a new life, brick by brick, in this new place I am now calling home. And that, truly, is invaluable.

CONCLUSION

The story of humanity is woven with the constant motif of migration, a reflection of our innate desire to seek what lies beyond the horizon, explore the unknown, and build a future that is forged by our own hands. "New Dawn, A Different Sky" has attempted to capture just a fraction of the vibrant, elaborate, and often heart-wrenching stories that comprise the immigrant experience. From the primal pang of leaving home to the arduous journey across borders, from the complexities of navigating a new language and culture to the quiet triumphs of building a life in unfamiliar surroundings, these narratives offer a glimpse into the resilience, courage, and unrelenting aspirations that define the immigrant spirit.

We have journeyed alongside individuals who left behind everything they knew, driven by dreams of opportunity, safety, or simply a chance to thrive. We have witnessed their struggles – the loneliness, the discrimination, the bureaucratic hurdles – and we have marvelled at their strength in the face of adversity. We have seen families torn apart and reunited, traditions preserved and adapted, and new identities forged in the crucible of cultural exchange. These stories are not just about overcoming obstacles; they are about the enduring human capacity for love, perseverance, and the pursuit of a better tomorrow.

The story of immigration is ongoing, with every new person weaving their distinct note into its constantly growing melody.

The challenges remain, but so too does the resilience, the hope, and the unwavering belief in the possibility of a new dawn under a different sky. It is our collective responsibility, as members of a global community, to create a world where every immigrant, regardless of their background or circumstance, is welcomed, respected, and given the opportunity to flourish.

Let these stories serve as a call to empathy, a monument to our shared humanity, and an inspiration to build bridges of understanding and compassion. Let us celebrate the richness that immigration brings to our societies, recognising that diversity is not just a point of contention but a source of advantage and innovation. And let us commit ourselves to creating a future where every individual, regardless of where they come from, can find their place under the sun and contribute their unique talents to the world. The journey continues, our collective narrative grows, and the dawn of a truly inclusive and equitable world awaits.

Final Thoughts

The journey of immigration is not easy. It demands sacrifice, toughness, and an unyielding spirit. But it also offers the potential for profound growth, both for the individual immigrant and for the societies that welcome them. Immigrants bring with them not only their skills and talents, but also their unique perspectives, enriching the cultural landscape and contributing to the dynamism of their new homes. As we move forward, it is imperative that we foster a greater degree of empathy and understanding towards immigrant communities.

We must actively work against prejudice and discrimination, advocate for just and equitable policies, and create welcoming spaces where all individuals, regardless of their origin, can feel safe, valued, and empowered to reach their full potential.

"New Dawn, A Different Sky" is not an ending, but rather a beginning. It is an invitation to continue the conversation, to deepen our understanding, and to commit to building a world where every individual, regardless of where they were born, has the opportunity to experience the promise of a new dawn and find their place under a different sky. The future of our communities, and indeed, the future of our world, depends on it.

ACKNOWLEDGEMENT

The completion of this book was made possible by the generous contributions of numerous individuals. I am tremendously grateful to my wife, Ateseme Cynthia Thompson, for her steadfast support, patience, and encouragement throughout this endeavour. I extend my sincere thanks to Iulia Tutomir for her insightful guidance and the dedication of her time.

I also wish to acknowledge Sulaiman Yusufu for his pioneering inspiration, Alessandro Verrós for his impartial critique, Alex Osmand for his motivational encouragement, Jeffrey Clement for his unwavering support and emotional intelligence, William F. Cooper for his constructive influence, Martin Jordan for his generous listening and insightful conversations, and Patrick Daley for his consistent concern and support.

Finally, I express my gratitude to all those who have contributed to my personal and intellectual growth, shaping both myself and this work.

ABOUT THE AUTHOR

Lawrence Thompson stands as a compelling voice in the realm of personal development, deeply rooted in the conviction that authentic and lasting growth is not externally imposed, but rather, organically cultivated from the fertile ground of one's inner self. He does not simply offer superficial self-help advice; instead, Thompson employs an exceptionally insightful and often introspective approach to guide readers on a transformative journey. His work is characterised by a keen understanding of the human psyche and the subtle yet powerful forces that shape our perceptions and behaviours.

In essence, Lawrence Thompson's work is a compelling invitation to embark on an inward journey of self-discovery and empowerment. He offers a nuanced and insightful roadmap for those seeking not just superficial success, but deep, meaningful, and enduring personal growth rooted in the belief that the most profound transformations begin from within.